ALSO BY JONATHAN COTT

Stockhausen: Conversations with the Composer

He Dreams What Is Going on Inside His Head (Ten Years of Writing)

City of Earthly Love (poems)

Forever Young (Conversations with Oriana Fallaci, Glenn Gould, Henry
    Miller, Walter Lowenfels, Werner Herzog, Stéphane Grappelli, and
    Maurice Sendak)

Charms (poems)

Pipers at the Gates of Dawn: The Wisdom of Children's Literature

Dylan

Conversations with Glenn Gould

The Search for Omm Sety

Visions and Voices (Conversations with Peter Brook, Oliver Sacks,
    Marie-Louise von Franz, George Balanchine, Pierre Boulez, Carolyn
    Forché, Sam Shepard, Bob Dylan, Federico Fellini, Lawrence
    Kushner)

Wandering Ghost: The Odyssey of Lafcadio Hearn

Isis and Osiris

Thirteen: A Journey into the Number

Homelands (poems)

Back to a Shadow in the Night: Music Writings and Interviews: 1968–2001

EDITED BY JONATHAN COTT

Beyond the Looking Glass: An Anthology of Victorian Fairy Tale
    Novels, Stories, and Poems

The Roses Race Around Her Name: Poems from Fathers to Daughters

Wonders: Writings for Children (co-editor)

The Ballad of John and Yoko (co-editor)

Masterworks of Children's Literature: 1550–1900

Victorian Color Picture Books

Skies in Blossom: The Nature Poetry of Emily Dickinson

ON THE SEA OF
MEMORY

ON THE SEA OF
MEMORY

A Journey from Forgetting to Remembering

JONATHAN COTT

Random House
New York

Published in the United States by Random House, an imprint of The Random House
Publishing Group, a division of Random House, Inc., New York.

RANDOM HOUSE and colophon are registered trademarks of Random House, Inc.

Grateful acknowledgment is made to the following:

Hyperion, for permission to reprint an excerpt from *Pass Thru Fire* by
Lou Reed. Copyright © 2000 by Lou Reed. Reprinted by permission of Hyperion.
All rights reserved.

Coleman Barks, for permission to reprint an excerpt from his translation of "Sublime
Generosity" by Rumi. Copyright © Coleman Barks.

Carcanet Press, for permission to reprint an excerpt from "A Kiss on the Head," from
Selected Poems by Marina Tsvetaeva, translated by Elaine Feinstein, copyright © 1971,
1981 by Elaine Feinstein. Published in the United States by Dutton,
a division of Penguin Group (USA). Reprinted by permission of Carcanet Press,
Manchester, England.

Library of Congress Cataloging-in-Publication Data

Cott, Jonathan.
On the sea of memory : a journey from forgetting to remembering / Jonathan Cott.
        p.   cm.
ISBN 1-4000-6058-3
1. Cott, Jonathan.   2. Memory disorders—Patients—Biography.   3. Memory
disorders—Patients—Rehabilitation.   4. Electroconvulsive therapy—Complications.
5. Memory.   I. Title.

RC394.M46C68 2005
362.196'1685'232092—dc22
[B]
2004062895

Printed in the United States of America on acid-free paper

www.atrandom.com

246897531

First Edition

Book design by Mercedes Everett

To Mnemosyne
and
to my friends who remind me who I was

The Teutonic god Odin had two pet ravens
called Thought and Memory. Each morning at
dawn he sent the ravens forth to circle the earth to
find out what had been going on. Each evening
they returned to roost and spent the night
recounting to Odin everything they'd seen and heard.
Then one day Odin started to wonder, What if
only one of the ravens returned? Which one could
he live without? And he understood that he could
live without Thought but not without Memory.

A Norse Story

ABC's *Good Morning America* seemed to score
the newsmaker interview of the week with
Diane Sawyer's exclusive televised chat with
Elian González. . . . In the presence of a psychoanalyst
the six-year-old boy recounted how he was saved
by dolphins when the boat that was carrying him,
his mother, and eleven other people from Cuba
to Florida sank. The boy told Ms. Sawyer that
he believed his mother, who drowned, had
survived the disaster but had not found him
because she had lost her memory.

The New York Times,
November 25, 1999

Contents

PREFACE

The brain, a walnut-surfaced, gelatinous, three-pound mass of protoplasm with the consistency of an overripe avocado, is the world of our being. More accurately and truly, the universe of our being. Containing approximately 100 billion neurons or nerve cells—more than there are stars in our galaxy—it has been called by James Watson (codiscoverer of DNA's double helix) "the last and greatest biological frontier" and "the most complex thing we have yet discovered in our universe." More than 32 million years would be required to count all the synapses—the channels of communication between nerve cells—in the human brain at a counting rate of one synapse per second. In his resplendent memoir *Speak, Memory*, Vladimir Nabokov put it this way: "How small the cosmos (a kangaroo's pouch would hold it), how paltry and puny in comparison to human consciousness, to a single individual recollection, and its expression in words!"

The neurologist Joseph LeDoux once commented that the brain is "just a piece of meat that has chemical and electrical charges" and that "to the extent that we are a product of our genes and experiences, we are our synapses." Those who believe the self is, among other things, social, psychological, moral, and aesthetic rather than neural in nature and who have experienced the ineffability and the numinous essence of both our universe and our inner selves might note, however, that LeDoux proposes his synaptic theory of the self not as an alternative to those other views but rather as a way to portray the manner in which the various aspects of the self are realized. Let us remember William Blake, who wrote: "For every thing that lives is holy." Neurons are holy. Synapses are holy. Axons and dendrites—our nerve fibers—are holy. The brain is holy. Walt Whitman said it beautifully:

> I accept Reality and dare not question it,
> Materialism first and last imbuing.
>
> Hurrah for positive science! long live exact demonstration! . . .
>
> Gentlemen! to you the first honors always!
> Your facts are useful and real—and yet they are not my dwelling,
> (I but enter by them to an area of my dwelling.)

Within our dwelling resides memory, one of the mysteries of the universe. Shakespeare called memory the "warder of the mind." It is the definer and preserver of one's identity and sense of self. We remember, therefore we are. In *Spiritual Dimensions of Psychology*, the Sufi teacher Hazrat Inayat Khan writes: "A person may lose his memory, but it does not lose him because the memory is one's own being." I disagree. Without memory, it is exactly one's being that is erased. In the *Zohar* (the Kabbalist *Book of Splendor*) it is stated: "A dream that is not remembered might as well not have been dreamt."

Without memory, you might as well have been asleep.

Without memory, it is as if your life had not been lived or as if someone else had lived it.

Without memory, it is difficult to discover who you were and who you really are.

Without memory, it is difficult to know who the person was who is the *you* whom you cannot now remember.

Without memory, you lose touch with yourself and the narrative of your life.

Without memory, you lose the human connectivity of previous experiences shared with others.

Without memory, you cannot recollect and reconnect to the feelings, of both joy and sorrow, that you once experienced.

Without memory, it is hard to feel a sense of responsibility for your forgotten past actions.

Without memory, it is hard to amalgamate past and present in order to carry on into the future.

Without memory, you experience the inner and outer worlds as places of disarrangement and disconnection.

Without memory, you are adrift and lost.

Having recently and permanently lost fifteen defining years of my life, from 1985 to 2000, after receiving numerous electroshock treatments—a procedure that many persons believe is no longer in use—I began, as I had never done before, to think seriously about memory (and its loss) and decided to undertake a journey into the worlds of forgetting and remembering. And in the course of my explorations, I began to think about different aspects of memory and was fortunate in my journey to encounter and interview a number of remarkable persons expert in subjects that have interested and fascinated me: the recent neuroscientific discoveries concerning memory and the brain (Richard Restak); the debate about false and recovered memories (Richard J. McNally); the connections between and among memory, imagination, and the soul (Thomas Moore); the possibilities of memory enhancement (Cynthia R. Green); the desire to erase one's memories (James L. McGaugh); the recollection of past lives from the Tibetan Buddhist perspective (Sogyal Rinpoche); the idea of remembrance in the Jewish tradition (Lawrence Kushner); the idea of Divine Remembrance in the Sufi tradition (Robert Frager); the role of the African griot or storyteller in recollecting and preserving the history of the African tribe (Judith Gleason); the idea of emotional memory in the teachings of Constantin Stanislavski (Ellen Burstyn); the devastating loss of memory from Alzheimer's disease (David Shenk). And I conclude my journey with some personal afterthoughts, including a conversation with a remarkable writer named Floyd Skloot, who suffered brain damage after contracting a virus on an airplane, whose debilitating neurological symptoms mirror my own, and with whom I developed a relationship as brothers-in-arms.

The poet Robert Duncan wrote: "There are memories everywhere then. Remembered, we go out, as in the first poem, upon the sea of night—to the drifting." Drifting on a sea of forgetfulness, I will always remember that memory is a saving gift. "Memories and emotions are fragile things," the blind French Resistance leader Jacques Lusseyran stated in *And There Was Light.* "You should never bear down on them or draw on them by main force. You should barely touch them with the tips of your fingers, the tips of your dreams." And I have ineluctably learned that one should never take this frangible and evanescent gift for granted.

PART ONE

FORGETTING

Yes, there were times when I forgot not only
who I was, but that I was, forgot to be.

Samuel Beckett,
Molloy

CHAPTER ONE

How I Lost My Memory

Something must have happened on May 4, 1998, because from that day forward my entire life changed. Since I don't remember what occurred, a Spanish friend of mine, Isa, who was visiting from Madrid and staying at my apartment in New York City, recalled the following:

"You came to Madrid in February 1998 and went several times to see a psychic who guided you in a kind of séance and put you in touch with your mother [who had died three years previously] in order to break the imprisoning bonds between you and her. I came with you each time to translate for you; and you cried and said good-bye to your mother, and you seemed much happier after this.

"Three months later I visited you in New York, and one morning you woke up and said, 'Why are you here? Why are you here?' I didn't understand, because you had always been a very good friend to me. And then you started shaking uncontrollably. So I went out and bought you some Bach Flowers, but you didn't want to take them, and finally you called a doctor who told you to go to the hospital.

"I went to visit you every day. They were giving you electroshock treatments—I didn't even know they still gave shock treatments—which I was against, and I spoke to the doctors. But they said you needed the treatments. One day when I came to the hospital I noticed that almost overnight your hair had turned gray. Everything was very strange. But you looked as if you had so much light in you. It was as if your soul was very spiritual but it was your ego that wasn't. Your ego was depressed and maniacal, but your soul was full of light. Maybe the psychic in Madrid opened up something that was too much for you to take."

Between 1998 and 1999 I was a patient in four New York City hospitals, suffering from major depression and suicidal thoughts. At the first two of these hospitals I underwent a course of thirty-six treatments of electroconvulsive therapy. ECT, or electroshock, entails sending an electrical current of about 200 volts—though sometimes less or more than that—for a fraction of a second by means of electrodes connected to a machine resembling a stereo receiver through the frontal lobes of the brain of a patient who has received general anesthesia and a muscle relaxant to prevent broken bones, cracked vertebrae, and physical spasms (the only perceivable movement during the treatment is usually the slight, involuntary twitching of the patient's toes); a face and nose mask to provide oxygen to the brain; and a rubber block to prevent biting off his or her tongue. The result is the creation of a grand mal epileptic seizure that lasts up to one minute. (Remarkably, it is still not known how or why ECT works or what the convulsion actually does to the brain.)

In the popular imagination, the prototypical electroshock patient brings to mind Randle P. McMurphy (who thought of ECT as "a device that might be said to do the work of the sleeping pill, the electric chair, and the torture rack"), the antihero of Ken Kesey's 1962 novel, One Flew over the Cuckoo's Nest, a book drawing on his experiences working in a psychiatric ward in an Oregon state mental hospital in the 1950s. Like McMurphy, ECT recipients at that time, as Sandra G. Boodman observes in The Washington Post, tended to be under forty, male, and impoverished—patients confined to state mental hospitals, often against their will. But women, of course, were also sufferers of this then often misused procedure. In the late 1940s and early 1950s, the internationally renowned writer Janet Frame, misdiagnosed without formal interviews or tests as a schizophrenic, underwent more than two hundred electroshock (including a few insulin shock) treatments over eight years, without an anesthetic, in two New Zealand hospitals where patients lived in rooms covered in human feces and ate meals off the floor. The treatments triggered extreme memory loss, comas, convulsions, and nightmares ("I dreamed waking and sleeping dreams more terrible than any I [had] dreamed before. . . . Everything tortured me and was on fire"). The doctors benightedly deduced that these symptoms indicated the need for further ECT. In *The Bell Jar*, published in 1963, Sylvia Plath describes her harrowing experiences with electroshock, also administered without an anesthetic, in the 1950s: "Then something beat down and took hold of me," she writes, "and shook me like the end of the world. Whee-ee-ee it shrilled, through an air crackling with blue light, and with each flash a great jolt drubbed me till I thought my bones would break and the sap fly out of me like a split plant. I wondered what terrible thing it was that I had done."

Incredibly and often ludicrously, ECT was once also used as a sedative to control disruptive patients as well as to treat ulcers, hysteria, colitis, backaches, psoriasis, phobias, anorexia nervosa, mental retardation, marital discord, and abhorrently, homosexuality—electroshock was supposed to "release" sexual impulses! The most notorious and egregiously baleful misuse of ECT occurred in the late 1950s and early 1960s, when Dr. Ewen Cameron, at one time the president of both the Canadian and American Psychiatric Associations, performed ghoulish experiments at McGill University's Allan Memorial Institute (since closed) in Montreal. In these Cold War experiments—part of the infamous "MK ULTRA" program subsidized by the CIA—which were meant to explore the processes and possibilities of brainwashing, Cameron, like the nefarious scientist in *The Manchurian Candidate*, maimed and brutalized patients with drugs (including LSD), lobotomies, and especially ECT (he would shock his patients six times in rapid succession two or three times a day for thirty days) in an attempt to discover ways of "depatterning" and then using "dynamic implants" (via tapes placed under the patients' pillows) to reprogram the human mind. His experiments were disastrous, resulting in individuals in vegetative states, with wiped out memories and the ability merely to repeat the sentence "I am at ease with myself." (Canadian survivors of this torture obtained and shared a $750,000 settlement from the U.S. government in 1988.)

Today electroshock is no longer applied for such barbaric purposes. ECT treatments are now given annually to an estimated 100,000 Americans (mostly women)—nearly triple the number in 1980—to alleviate mental illnesses such as major depression (women are often treated for postnatal or menopausal depression), mania, catatonia, and some forms of schizophrenia, primarily as a last resort, when other treatments, such as psychotherapy, psychoactive drugs, and hospitalization, have failed. The cost per treatment of ECT ranges from $300 to $1,000; and as the Tampa psychiatrist Dr. Walter E. Afield, a former consultant to Johns Hopkins Hospital and a supporter of ECT, comments somewhat grimly, "Insurers no longer will pay psychiatrists to do psychotherapy, but they will pay for shock or for medical tests. . . . Finances are dictating the treatment. . . . We're being pushed as a specialty to do what's going to pay."

Using electricity to heal people goes back at least two thousand years. In the first century A.D., Roman healers applied electric eels to the heads of both mentally disturbed persons and those whom today we would say were suffering from migraine. Physicians in the eighteenth and nineteenth centuries used electrical generators whose charge was built up by electroluminescence (resulting from rubbing a rotating ball of sulfur) on their patients, claiming efficacious results in the treatment of various mental disorders. But the modern use of ECT began in Rome in 1938, when Dr. Ugo Cerletti, chief of the Clinic for Nervous and Mental Diseases at the University of Rome, in collaboration with Dr. Lucio Bini, adapted a pair of tongs used to stun hogs before slaughter and applied them to the temples of a delirious and delusional thirty-nine-year-old homeless man who was found wandering in a train station spouting gibberish. As the psychiatrist David Impasto, who administered the first electroshock treatment in the United States in 1940, wrote: "After the electric spasm, the patient burst into song. Cerletti suggested that another treatment with a higher voltage be given. The patient suddenly sat up and pontifically proclaimed, no longer in jargon but in clear Italian, 'Not again! It will kill me!' This made the professor think and swallow, but his courage was not lost . . . and the first electroconvulsion in man ensued."

In 2001 the New York State Assembly Committee on Mental Health, chaired by Martin A. Luster, scheduled two public hearings—in New York City on May 18 and in Albany on July 18—to determine the efficacy, benefits, and risks of ECT. According to the committee's report, "It was clear from the testimony received that there was a wide variation of opinion related to the use of ECT. Proponents claimed that ECT is a safe, effective procedure with no permanent adverse side effects, and cited a figure of 1 in 10,000 deaths related to ECT to document its safety. [The American Psychiatric Association Committee on ECT in a 2001 report claims one death occurs for every 80,000 treatments.] In contrast, opponents maintained that ECT causes brain damage, can result in permanent memory loss, and asserted that the death rate related to ECT was closer to 1 in 200. Opponents expressed additional concerns about the utilization of ECT on children, the elderly, other vulnerable populations, and of its possible use as a behavior-modifying, non-therapeutic intervention for mentally retarded individuals." The committee report also mentions that although the Food and Drug Administration has recognized the risk of illness or injury from ECT and has designated and classified ECT machines as Class III medical devices—a designation used for premarket approval for equipment that shows an unreasonable risk of illness or injury—the FDA has never completed testing ECT devices to determine their safety or the effects of ECT on the brain, and there is currently no regulation of ECT by the federal government.

Even taking into account that some memory loss can result from stress, depression, and aging, what I know for certain is that after thirty-six electroshock treatments, innumerable memories have been literally and permanently erased, with only occasional freeze-framed flashbacks. Neuroscientists have confirmed that strong emotions, which release adrenaline, which activates the brain, make for emotionally charged memories, often called "flashbulb memories." One such memory for me is of the night in December 1994 when I found myself lost in the Sahara Desert in Niger and had to spend fourteen hours alone until I was found by my party's Tuareg guides.

I have discovered that I have totally forgotten persons I used to know well: a friend told me that after my ECT treatments, I telephoned her, mentioned that I had come across her name in my address book, and asked, "Who are you?" And I have also found my explicit, short-term memory debilitated, my IQ quantifiably diminished (attested to by extensive neuropsychological assessments), my abstract reasoning and learning facility (such as trying for an ungodly number of hours to figure out how to work a new phone-fax machine or how to accomplish simple computer tasks) seriously impaired, my ability to find the words I want and need reduced (such that I struggle to write more than four or five sentences at a time and have to compensate for the loss of words I mean with simpler and less precise ones), and my cognitive capabilities weakened to the extent that I immediately forget what I've just read, even losing track of the meanings of the words.

The singer-poet Lou Reed, who underwent electroshock treatments to "cure" his homosexuality at a New York state mental hospital in 1961, when he was seventeen, shares my reading plight in the first stanza of his song "Kill Your Sons": "All your two-bit psychiatrists / Are giving you electroshock / They said they'd let you live at home with mom and dad / Instead of mental hospitals / But every time you tried to read a book / You couldn't / Get to page seventeen / 'Cause you forgot where you were / So you couldn't even read." And a few hours or a day after I watch a movie, I find myself unable to recollect most of what I've seen. First I realize that I have forgotten the film's ending, then its middle, and finally its beginning, like a kind of retrograde process of film erosion. (Even as I type these pages, I often lose track of what I've just written, and I search for words I no longer remember. Sometimes an unbeckoned word or phrase will come suddenly to my mind—for example, "the exactitude of pain," which popped into my head a few minutes before writing this sentence. Sometimes I am overjoyed to catch a needed word like a fisherman with his net in a sea of forgetfulness. Someone once said that memory is like the ocean because from memory flow all thoughts and words. I am truly at a loss for words.)

While I clearly remember the smallest details of my early childhood—sitting under the piano at the age of four or five listening to my mother play Chopin's Prelude in A Major, for example, or sitting next to a blond-haired, narcoleptic eight-year-old girl named Betty, who continually used to fall asleep, head on her desk, when we were in the third grade—many of my later years have been almost totally expunged. In a significant study undertaken in 1974, the psychiatrist and neuroscientist Dr. Larry R. Squire tested psychiatric patients before and after ECT treatments on their memory of television shows. Before ECT, these patients exhibited a good memory for programs from the late sixties and early seventies, though not for shows before those years; after ECT, however, they had trouble remembering programs aired a year or two before ECT but almost no problems remembering shows from more remote time periods. In neurological terms, as Joseph LeDoux writes in *Synaptic Self,* "damage to the hippocampus [the horseshoe-shaped part of the brain where memory is initially encoded] affects recent memories, but not old ones that have already been consolidated in the cortex. Old memories are the result of accumulations of synaptic changes in the cortex as a result of multiple reinstatements of the memory."

There have been notable attempts to forbid the use of ECT. In 1982 voters in Berkeley, California, passed a referendum banning the treatment, although the law was subsequently overturned by a suit brought by the American Psychiatric Association (an unequivocal and adamant advocate for ECT). And in 1991 the Board of Supervisors in San Francisco adopted a resolution opposing the use of electroshock. In 1997 a bill that would have made administering ECT a criminal act, punishable by a fine of up to $10,000 and/or up to six months in jail, was narrowly defeated in Texas.

In this regard, one has to mention the mission (more accurately, the crusade) undertaken by the controversial Citizens Commission on Human Rights to ban ECT everywhere in the world. Founded in 1969 by the Church of Scientology "to investigate and expose psychiatric violations of human rights," the commission is separately incorporated and has offices in forty states and chapters in thirty other countries. Along with its lobbying of state and foreign governments to ban ECT, the commission publishes pamphlets and information letters that read like manifestos but are often based on reliable facts about the dangers of ECT and the misrepresentations of some of its practitioners. I must note that it also attacks with paranoid abandon the entire psychiatric profession ("Psychiatry: A Human Rights Abuse and Global Failure," "Psychiatry Harming Lives: Betraying and Drugging Children," "Psychiatry Victimizing the Elderly," "Psychiatry's Creation of Racism") as well as the use of ECT ("Therapy or Torture?" "Shock from Birth to Grave," "Apartheid and ECT," "The Nazi Heritage—'Electroshock's development . . . traces back to a dark alliance between psychiatry and the Nazi concentration camps'").

Impossible as it is to go along with this take-no-prisoners approach (the psychiatric profession is one that attempts to help and heal people, obviously does much good, and is hardly "a human rights abuse"), one has to acknowledge that the Citizens Commission on Human Rights has some positive accomplishments to its credit, such as pressuring the California legislature to prohibit ECT for patients under age twelve (some major teaching hospitals have begun to use the treatment on children as young as eight) and influencing the Texas legislature to make that state the most difficult in the nation in which to receive ECT treatment. In any case, it is generally acknowledged that the commission has called the widespread practice of ECT into question and put psychiatrists and ECT practitioners on the defensive.

The proponents of ECT, however, are still an extraordinarily powerful and influential group in the psychiatric community. One of the treatment's leading advocates, Max Fink, a professor of psychiatry at the State University of New York at Stonybrook, one of six ECT experts who served on the American Psychiatric Association's 1990 task force that drafted guidelines for the treatment, and the author of *Electroshock: Restoring the Mind*, has stated: "ECT is one of God's gifts to mankind. There is nothing like it, nothing to equal it in efficacy or safety in all of psychiatry. . . . ECT is the most effective antidepressant, antipsychotic, anticatatonic we have today." (In a manner strangely reminiscent of Citizens Commission hyperbole, Fink likened the article "Electroshock: The Unkindest Therapy of All" by Fred Hapgood in the January 1980 issue of *The Atlantic Monthly*, which in spite of its provocative title is sober, reasoned, and thoroughly researched, to *Mein Kampf!*)

An editorial in the March 2001 issue of the *Journal of the American Medical Association* states: "The results of ECT in treating severe depression are among the most positive treatment effects in all of medicine. . . . For the sake of the many patients with major depression and their families, it is time to bring ECT out of the shadows." The psychiatrist T. George Bidder has written that ECT has "a therapeutic efficacy, in properly selected cases, comparable to some of the most potent and specific treatments available, such as penicillin in pneumococcal pneumonia." Richard Abrams, the cofounder and co-owner of Somatics, which *The Washington Post* reports manufactures at least half of the ECT machines sold worldwide at nearly $10,000 apiece, is at the same time the author of psychiatry's most comprehensive and standard textbook on electroshock, *Electroconvulsive Therapy* (now in its fourth edition). In it he writes: "There is simply no evidence—and virtually no chance—that ECT as presently administered is capable of producing brain damage."

Richard Weiner, professor of psychiatry at the Duke University Medical Center, who represented the American Psychiatric Association before the New York State Assembly Committee on Mental Health, stated:

Major psychiatric textbooks agree that, despite an ever increasing number of alternative treatments, ECT remains the most rapid and effective treatment of major depression, and also that it is efficacious in selected individuals with mania and schizophrenia. The effectiveness and speed of action of ECT are particularly valuable commodities, given the demonstrated high mortality and morbidity of these conditions, not only from the direct effects of the mental illness, e.g., suicide, anorexia, inanition, and general debilitation, but also from medical disorders of many types, including cardiovascular disease, which are significantly more likely and more severe in individuals suffering from these conditions. Serious mental disorders, particularly of the type and severity that typically leads to a referral for ECT, are bad for one's health and shorten one's lifespan.

One of the most influential proponents and practitioners of ECT is Harold Sackheim, a onetime consultant to MECTA Corporation (an ECT machine manufacturer), a member (like Fink) of the American Psychiatric Association's six-member ECT Task Force, and chief of biological psychiatry at the New York State Psychiatric Institute in New York City (where I received twenty-six of my ECT treatments as part of an ongoing multimillion-dollar research study funded by the National Institute of Mental Health). In his written testimony to the New York State Assembly Committee on Mental Health, Dr. Sackheim stated:

> The efficacy of ECT in specific psychiatric conditions is amongst the most well established of any treatment in all of medicine. . . . During and following ECT, patients will show rapid forgetting of newly learned information. This is termed anterograde amnesia. All available information, from scores of studies, indicates that this deficit disappears within days to a few weeks following the receipt of the treatment. . . . All recent published surveys of patients who have received ECT have shown that the vast majority report that this form of memory loss is a small price to pay for the therapeutic effects of the treatment. As with all medical treatments, there are individual differences, and some very rare

patients may manifest more extensive memory loss. There is no firm estimate on this incidence but my estimate would be on the order of 1 in 500 patients. Careful scientific study has shown that ECT does not cause brain damage (cellular death).

It is significant that Sackheim, who has always insisted that ECT memory dysfunction is "strongly associated" with "the severity of depressive symptoms," and has even suggested that subjective memory can "improve" following ECT, has recently acknowledged that memory and cognitive losses associated with ECT are real, admitting to *The Atlantic Monthly* in 2001 that "the field has been under attack for such a long period of time that a defensive posture was developed where limitations of the treatment were not acknowledged. So people complained of profound cognitive effects, and [those effects] were attributed to an ongoing psychopathology and essentially dismissed. I think that hurt the field of ECT."

On the other side of the ECT debate, the neurobiologist Steven Rose in *The Conscious Brain* states that "the neurological rationale [for ECT] is obscure, to say the least. Putting an electrical current through the head undoubtedly temporarily affects the electrical properties of most of the neurons; there are sharp biochemical changes in the level of glucose and its metabolites; oxygen consumption, protein syntheses, and many other parameters are affected as well. Some, presumably random, cell death must occur. The treatment is analogous to attempting to mend a faulty radio by kicking it, or a broken computer by cutting out a few of its circuits. Even accepting the therapeutic value of electroshock, it is difficult to believe that so massive and crude a treatment will ever be able to tell us much about the neurobiological bases for the disturbances it claims to cure."

In the September 1977 issue of *The American Journal of Psychiatry*, the neurologist John M. Friedberg concludes that ECT may result in brain damage, and writes this of the ECT-induced grand mal seizure and of its aftermath: "A tetanic muscular contraction, the 'electric spasm,' is followed after a latency of seconds by unconsciousness, a high voltage paroxysmal spike and sharp-wave discharge, and a clonic convulsion. Upon recovery of consciousness the subject is left with a transient acute brain syndrome, a high likelihood of permanent brain damage, and greater retrograde amnesia [in which people have difficulty remembering experiences that occurred before strokes and head injuries] than is seen in any other form of head injury."

And one of the most outspoken critics of ECT is Peter Sterling, a neuroscientist in the Department of Neuroscience at the University of Pennsylvania. In his testimony before the New York State Assembly Committee on Mental Health, he stated:

> ECT unquestionably damages the brain, and there are a variety of mechanisms that lead to this damage. In the first place, the electroshock delivered to the skull is basically similar to what you would get out of an electrical wall outlet, except that there is a transformer in the ECT machine that steps up the voltage. When this is done two or three times a week for weeks, it's just completely obvious that this is going to eventually cause some kind of brain damage. Second, ECT causes grand mal epileptic seizures, and this causes an acute rise in blood pressure, well into the hypertensive range. And it frequently causes small hemorrhages in the brain. Wherever a hemorrhage occurs in the brain, nerve cells die, and they are not replaced. A third thing that ECT does is to rupture the blood brain barrier. This barrier normally protects the brain from potentially damaging substances in the blood. Breaching this barrier also leads to swelling of the brain, and swelling leads to local arrest of blood supply, to loss of oxygen, and to death of neurons. The fourth thing is that ECT causes neurons to release large quantities of glutamate. Glutamate excites further neuronal activity, and this becomes a vicious cycle. Neurons literally kill themselves from overactivity, and the key manifestation of this brain damage is retrograde memory loss. . . . Virtually all patients experience some degree of persistent and, likely, permanent retrograde amnesia.

There are many other witnesses to this kind of deleterious and permanent long-term, as well as short-term, memory loss. In his remarkable study of depression, *The Noonday Demon*, Andrew Solomon writes of a practicing lawyer who came out of ECT without any recollection of having attended law school. She was unable to remember anything she had studied, where she had studied, or whom she had known during her studies. The poet John Wieners, who spoke fluent French, was no longer able to speak or understand the language after receiving shock treatments. There have also been reports of persons who forgot they had children or, to give a less dramatic example, a woman who couldn't remember her own clothing and demanded to know who had put the unfamiliar dresses in her closet.

Most ironic and telling is the remark of one psychiatrist that psychotherapy was useless in patients undergoing ECT because they couldn't remember "either the analyst or the content of the analytic sessions from one day to the next." The New York City–based Committee for Truth in Psychiatry—a loose-knit national organization of ECT survivors—has collected hundreds of personal testimonies of similar devastating memory and cognitive loss, some of which were entered into the New York State Assembly Committee on Mental Health report. These are voices unacknowledged by most of the psychiatric profession. For example:

> Nearly 20 years ago I underwent 30 shock treatments. As a result I lost two full years of memory. I have one child, a daughter, and the two years that were wiped out in my memory were the years when she was two and three years old; those memories are irreplaceable.

> I had to retire from part-time work as a paraprofessional in a local high school and I doubt I will ever be able to work again. I have forgotten how to weave, could not concentrate on anything, felt very little pleasure in life and still feel suicidal. I often don't remember people who speak to me, much of my past life is gone from my memory, I have cognitive thinking problems, fear being in any social situation, cannot spell, cannot remember factual information and live a rather hermit-like existence.

"Memory" isn't just a data bank of pieces of information. Memory pretty much covers everything we know and feel, and need to know and feel, to function—on every level. I lost knowledge, skills, abilities, and feelings of all kinds, and these losses made it impossible to function in work, routine activities, self-care, relationships, etc. . . . I am also having to re-learn *how* to remember—I lost the process itself of remembering and learning.

My doctor informed me that I would experience some short-term memory loss, but reassured me that my memory would return to normal within six weeks following the end of the treatments. He pronounced me "cured" and urged me to return to college. I had to drop out of school when I realized I could not remember what I had studied before entering the hospital, and I was totally unable to absorb new material. I suffered for many months from a complete inability to concentrate, and was not able to even read a newspaper or magazine. I have been left with permanent memory loss of events that preceded the ECT by several months.

It's been 7–8 years since I've had [ECT treatments], the long term damage is there and it's not coming back. At one time I never minded filling out job applications, I loved to read, my goal was to finish high school G.E.D. and become somebody. I can no longer fill out applications. I'm not able to retain anything I might learn, I read and the next minute it's gone, I can't follow written instructions, I become confused.

I had three shock treatments and for years after I could read a simple newspaper article over and over and still could not state what I had read. I still have terrible problems. . . . The treatments only gave a temporary relief from emotional pain, a day or two, and depression was right back as bad as ever.

Most of my life from 1975–1987 is a fog. I remember some things when reminded by friends, but other reminders remain a mystery. My best friend since high school in the 1960s died recently and with her went a big part of my life because she knew all about me and used to help me out with the parts I couldn't remember.

I haven't had a shock for over ten years now but I still feel sad that I can't remember most of my late childhood or any of my high school days. I can't even remember my first intimate experience. What I know of my life is secondhand. My family has told me bits and pieces and I have my high school yearbooks. But my family generally remembers the "bad" times, usually how I screwed up the family life, and the faces in the yearbook are all total strangers.

As a result of these "treatments" the years 1966–1969 are almost a total blank in my mind. In addition, the five years preceding 1966 are severely fragmented and blurred. My entire college education has been wiped out. I have no recollection of ever being at the University of Hartford. I know that I graduated from the institution because of a diploma I have which bears my name, but I do not remember receiving it. It has been ten years since I received electroshock and my memory is still as blank as it was the day I left the hospital. There is nothing temporary about the nature of memory loss due to electroshock. It is permanent, devastating, and irreparable.

ECT destroyed: (1) My health, (2) My marriage, (3) My family, (4) Our finances, (5) Our lives.

Another organization, ECT Anonymous, based in West Yorkshire, England, reports hundreds of cases of similar memory loss. In light of these testimonies, it is interesting to quote the words, presented on an educational video prepared by Somatics, of Dr. Max Fink: "Now when we give a patient treatment over three or four weeks they tend to have a fuzzy idea of what happened in the hospital, but [other than] the treatments themselves, the patients do not forget what happened in their early life, they don't forget what happened in their childhood, they don't forget the telephone, they don't forget the names of their children, they don't forget their work, and they have no difficulty in learning . . . after the treatment is over when they're better."

It is also interesting after reading the ECT survivors' testimonies to note the similarity between their words and a description of minor head injury in the National Head Injury Foundation brochure "The Unseen Injury: Minor Head Trauma": "Memory problems are common. . . . It may be harder to learn new information or routines. Your attention may be shorter, you may be easily distracted or forget things or lose your place when you have to shift back and forth confused, e.g., when reading. You may find it harder to find the right word or express exactly what you are thinking. You may think and respond more slowly, and it may take more effort to do the things you used to do automatically. You may not have the same insights or spontaneous ideas as you did before. . . . You may find it more difficult to make plans, get organized, and set and carry out realistic goals." (In the March 1983 issue of *Clinical Psychiatry News*, the neurologist and electro-encephalographer Sidney Sament writes that "after a few sessions of ECT, the symptoms are those of moderate cerebral contusion" and that "after multiple sessions of ECT, a patient has symptoms identical to those of a retired, punch-drunk boxer.")

Considering these testimonies, one might cast a skeptical eye on the patient information pamphlet published by Somatics, which states: "ECT does not interfere with the ability to learn, and many studies have shown better learning after ECT than before it, probably because of improved concentration from relief of depression. A few patients, however, still have not regained some specific personal memories when tested six months or longer after receiving a form of treatment called bilateral (temple-to-temple) ECT. [Bilateral ECT stimulates both sides of the brain; unilateral ECT stimulates only the right side of the brain, where memory is less affected.] Generally, these memories are for events in the months immediately preceding ECT. *No long term or persistent effects of ECT on intellectual abilities or memory capacity have been shown to occur*" (emphasis added). And one might note that in December 1960, after undergoing twenty

ECT treatments at the Mayo Clinic in Rochester, Minnesota, Ernest Hemingway wrote to his biographer A. E. Hotchner: "What is the sense of ruining my head and erasing my memory, which is my capital, and putting me out of business? It was a brilliant cure, but we lost the patient." A month later, after his last electroshock treatment, Hemingway fatally shot himself.

It is undeniable, however, that intractable depression, catatonia, mania, and some forms of schizophrenia can be alleviated by ECT (but often only temporarily, and always with some kind of memory loss). A counselor at a Boston mental hospital told me of a clinically depressed woman on her ward who when admitted had lost forty pounds and had to be fed by IV and who did not respond to seven different medications; the morning after receiving six ECT treatments she woke, sat up in bed smiling, and talked to her roommate about how she planned to take her camper and travel around the country. (One hopes she remembered where she parked the camper!) Shortly after the millennium, the New York State Assembly Committee on Mental Health heard testimony and received letters attesting to the benefits of ECT. One letter read: "I suffer from chronic depressive disorder and received ECT two years ago [1999]. . . . ECT has allowed me to function again. I will be eternally grateful that ECT was available to me and hope that it will continue to be available in the future."

In 1993 Dick Cavett recounted to *People* magazine that since 1959, when he graduated from Yale, he had been suffering periodic debilitating depressions. His worst depression occurred in May 1980, when he felt so agitated that he was taken off a London-bound Concorde jet and driven to New York's Columbia Presbyterian Hospital (one of my alma maters), where he was given ECT. "In my case ECT was miraculous," he said. "My wife was dubious, but when she came into my room afterward, I sat up and said, 'Look who's back among the living.' It was a magic wand." Cavett stayed in the hospital for six weeks and has stabilized himself by taking antidepressants ever since.

The National Depressive and Manic Depressive Association, an organization of psychiatric patients, supports the use of ECT, as does the National Alliance for the Mentally Ill, a lobbying

group composed of relatives of people with chronic mental illness. As Steven Rose notes in *The Conscious Brain*, "According to
the standards used in the evaluation of any treatment for 'mental
disorders,' [ECT] does often seem to work . . . that is, its use enables an individual to return to his or her . . . previous environment and function in a more adjusted way to it. Whether this is
desirable is another matter." In this regard, Rose agrees with
Plato, who in his Seventh Letter stated: "He who advises a sick
man, whose manner of life is prejudicial to health, is clearly
bound first of all to change his patient's manner of life, and if the
patient is willing to obey him, he may go on to give him other advice."

Because of the benefits that many people do receive from
ECT, I do not think that the treatment should be banned. I do,
however, believe that ECT should be used only as a last resort,
with as few treatments as possible, second opinions (perhaps, as
has been suggested, from psychiatrists who do not use ECT)
mandatory, and severe restrictions both on dangerous bilateral
treatments (where significant and devastating memory loss and
impairment of verbal and some nonverbal functions are confirmed by many studies) and on the application of levels of electricity far above the seizure threshold. Informing patients and
their families pro forma, as most ECT practitioners do, that in-
evitable short-term and possible long-term memory loss will
eventually be remitted—which is what my doctors told me—
contradicts the evidence of too many permanently fractured elec-
troshocked brains. (Patients in the throes of extreme mental
disturbance are in any case hardly able to consent to this procedure in any considered manner, and their families are almost always ignorant about ECT.) The model consent form drafted by
the American Psychiatric Association and copied by hospitals
claims that perhaps only 1 in 200 patients reports lasting memory
problems (Harold Sackheim suggests 1 in 500; both are unsub-
stantiated assessments), adding, "The reasons for these rare reports
of long-lasting memory impairment are not fully understood."
But even in a report published in 2001, the American Psychiatric
Association finally confronts for what is probably the first time in

its history the possibility of serious memory problems occasioned by ECT.

The pact with the devil that is ECT requires that one trade certain memory loss (short-term, long-term, or both), possible brain damage, and cognitive dysfunction for the temporary relief of depression. I say temporary because although a 1993 American Psychiatric Association fact sheet concludes that at least 80 percent of patients with intractable depression show substantial improvement after ECT, it does not mention that the relapse rate is high. Up to 50 percent of patients relapsed within six months of stopping ECT according to a 2001 study reported in the *Journal of the American Medical Association*—a fact not disclosed to patients in educational literature or consent forms. This is why growing numbers of psychiatrists are recommending monthly maintenance, or "booster," shock treatments, even though there is little evidence that these are effective. Moreover, a 1986 Indiana University study of 1,494 psychiatric patients found that those who committed suicide five to seven years after hospitalization were somewhat more likely to have had ECT than were those who died of other causes. The researchers, who also reviewed the literature on ECT and suicide, concluded that these findings "do not support the commonly held belief that ECT exerts long-range protective effects against suicide."

After examining the results of fifty-three studies conducted between 1975 and 2002 concerning the relationship between ECT and memory loss, I concluded that there were twenty-one demonstrations of significant memory loss from electroshock contrasted with thirteen attestations to few deleterious long-term effects and a sometime improvement of memory and concentration thanks to the amelioration of depression. (Many researchers have pointed out that depression and stress can impair memory by altering the functioning of the hippocampus.) The remaining nineteen studies presented mixed conclusions.

But it is worth noting the remarks of A. B. Donohue, a former lawyer and ex-ECT patient who lost about nine years of her memory, in *The Journal of ECT*: "The cause for the significant gap between research and anecdotal evidence regarding the extent of some memory loss after ECT has never been adequately explained. A patient's development of awareness and self-education about the severe side effects of ECT raises questions regarding many current assumptions about memory loss. ECT-specific studies, which conclude that side effects are short term and narrow in scope, have serious limitations, including the fact that they do not take into account broader scientific knowledge about memory function." Moreover, a small study in *Psychological Medicine* in 2003 reported that Spanish scientists have discovered that depressive patients receiving maintenance electroshock treatments experienced impairments in both short-term memory and frontal function as well as alterations in verbal fluency, mental flexibility, working memory, and visuomotor speed—all symptoms I share.

The lack of consensus regarding the effect of ECT on memory and cognitive function makes us anxiously await the day when devices like transcranial magnetic stimulators become commonly available. These stimulators use an intense magnetic field to produce therapeutic seizures that are significantly less intense than ECT seizures and that will be able to combat depression and other illnesses without the damaging side effects of memory loss (though with frequent headaches). Also promising is the still experimental use of EP-MRSI scans—a method of magnetic resonance imaging used to observe the effects of certain pharmaceuticals—on bipolar subjects, which seem, without side effects, to improve the mood of patients suffering from this disorder. As Michael Rohan at McLean Hospital in Belmont, Massachusetts, has stated: "It's only a first look and we need to stay realistic, but we're excited about its potential as a treatment for human depression."

WHAT DO I NOT REMEMBER? THE WORLD AS IT WAS (THE END OF the Cold War, the Oslo peace accords, the abolition of apartheid, the massacre at Srebrenica). Who was born and who died during my forgotten years. My friend Annie, who visited me one day in the hospital in 1998 accompanied by her daughter Sasha, recounts how I told them that I had seen a magazine that said it had been a year since Princess Diana had died. "And you looked up at me," Annie told me, "and said, 'Is that true, Princess Diana died, how did she die?' So I told you. And I realized that you didn't know which famous people were alive and which ones were dead. So I started to tell you people who had died whom I knew you loved: Glenn Gould, Sviatoslav Richter, Bob Marley, and when I told you that John Lennon had been killed, you wept. I felt as if I were murdering all these people for you."

Also completely forgotten are the films I saw or the contents of my favorite books read during the 1980s and '90s—Robert Musil's *The Man Without Qualities*, Halldór Laxness's *Independent People*, Andrei Platonov's *The Fierce and Beautiful World*, Kenzaburo Oe's *Teach Us to Outgrow Our Madness*. Fortunately, I have always been in the habit of marking passages that I find worth remembering in order to be able to return to them and reenter their worlds. As Emily Dickinson wrote of her similar habit: "I won't forget some little pencil marks I found in reading *Picciola*, for they seem to me like silent sentinels, guarding the towers of some city, in itself—too beautiful to be unguarded."

I have also forgotten engaging in research on and even writing the six books and the magazine articles I worked on as well as the four books I edited during these years (when I reread them now, they seem to have been written and edited by a different person) and everything having to do with the travels I undertook for these projects. I have lost my memories of places as diverse as Edmonton, Canada; County Carlow, Ireland; a small island in the Swedish archipelago; the rock and moss gardens in Kyoto, Japan; Chengdu, China (to visit the home of the great eighth-century poet Tu Fu); and Lhasa, Tibet, where I do not even remember the imposing Potala Palace. So I depend on photographs, postcards, letters from friends, my passport's visa stamps, even T-shirts and poems I wrote to confirm my existence in those places. Recently, I came upon a file in which I discovered two of my poems, one from Lhasa in 1993, the other from Cow Island in 1996, neither of which I recall having written. The former poem describes a procession of Tibetans carrying prayer flags:

ON THE TOP OF THE WORLD

On the top of the world
the birds have wings of silver

The sun shines
closer to your eyes

Every color is a prayer
blowing in the sky

People from afar appear
almost without moving

They wear radiant clothes
in a path of dust

There are bells
ringing on their wrists

They carry things
in their heart

Sometimes they look at you
behind your eyes

The light hurts
each breath gets smaller

In the pulsing of your blood
you can feel the turning of your lives

The latter describes waking up on Cow Island:

DAWN

Outside
into the sun:
no way to sleep,
no place to run away

•

Raising my arms:
a long, thin Giacometti shadow
amid the sleeping shadows of cows;
and beyond,
a blinding ultramarine sea
that is the shadow of the sky

•

Outside my cottage: An ancient, rectangular stone foundation of a
now non-existent house, inside of which is a tiny vegetable garden
enclosed in wire mesh, outside of which are small stones jutting up
from the earth like teeth, with dandelions and clover growing
about. Here is where I worship.

•

The bliss of standing alone at dawn,
of being a family at noontime,
a couple at midnight

•

Don't ever let me go back to sleep

These poems at least confirmed to me my presence in these two
faraway and now unfathomable places.

Perhaps the most arresting description I have read of this experiential sense of vacuum, uncannily mirroring my own, occurs in
Paul Auster's *The Locked Room*—the third novel in his New York
Trilogy—in which the narrator, obsessed by his missing childhood friend Fanshawe, finds himself in Paris investigating his
friend's past. He writes: "If I am able to say anything about this period at all, it is only because I have certain documentary evidence
to help me. The visa stamps in my passport, for example; my airplane ticket, my hotel bill, and so on. . . . I see things that happened, I encounter images of myself in various places, but only at
a distance, as though I were watching someone else. None of it
feels like memory, which is always anchored within; it's out there
beyond what I can feel or touch, beyond anything that has to do
with me."

Most unsettling are my forgotten meetings, encounters, and

relationships with friends and acquaintances both at home and in various parts of the world. People inform me of where we met, where we went, what we did, what we saw, what we said, what we thought, what we felt—everything, to my dismay, lost to me in the blur of forgotten time. Washington Irving's Rip Van Winkle, having lost his way in the Catskill Mountains, came across a crowd of little goblinlike men who proffered him a flagon containing a strange sleep-inducing brew. And like him, I fell asleep and woke up to find years of my life gone and almost everything in the world changed.

IN HIS BOOK *THE MAN WHO MISTOOK HIS WIFE FOR A HAT*, THE neurologist Oliver Sacks presents a case study entitled "The Lost Mariner," of a forty-nine-year-old man named Jimmie G., who was admitted to the Home for the Aged near New York City in 1975. Confused and disoriented, Jimmie G. greets Dr. Sacks with a "Hiya, Doc! Nice morning! Do I take this chair here?" He proceeds to tell him about his childhood in a small Connecticut town, recollecting the houses his family lived in, and even remembers his several phone numbers. He recalls his experiences as a navy submarine radio operator during World War II. Speaking in the past tense about his early childhood, Jimmie inexplicably uses the present tense to describe his days in the navy. "What year is this, Mr. G.?" Sacks asks him. "Forty-five, man," he replies. "What do you mean? We've won the war, FDR's dead, Truman's at the helm. There are great times ahead." Sacks then asks him his age, and Jimmie says, "Why, I guess I'm nineteen, Doc." Then, upon looking into a mirror and seeing his gray hair, he turns pale and whispers, "Christ, what's going on? What's happened to me? Is this a nightmare? Am I crazy? Is this a joke?" "It's okay, Jimmie," Sacks consoles him. "It's just a mistake. Nothing to worry about."

When Sacks steps out of the room, then returns a few minutes later, Jimmie, having forgotten the shock of self-recognition, exclaims: "Hiya, Doc! Nice morning! You want to talk to me—do I take this chair here?" "Haven't we met before, Mr. G.?" Sacks asks him. "No, I can't say we have. . . . I wouldn't forget *you*, Doc!" "Why do you call me 'Doc'?" Sacks asks. "I see these beds, and these patients everywhere. Looks like a sort of hospital to me. But hell, what would I be doing in a hospital—and with all these old people, years older than me. I feel good, I'm strong as a bull. Maybe I *work* here. . . . Do I work? What's my job? . . . No, you're shaking your head, I see in your eyes I don't work here. If I don't work here, I've been *put* here. Am I a patient, am I sick and don't know it, Doc? It's crazy, it's scary. . . . Is it some sort of joke?"

Cut off from his past after 1945, Jimmie G. is unable to form memories for more than a few seconds, unable to remember that he can't remember. As Sacks comments: If a person loses a self—himself—he cannot know it because he is no longer there to know it. Sacks surmises that Jimmie G. suffered a massive cerebral or emotional trauma in the war but also points to similarities between this type of memory loss and the effects of Korsakoff's syndrome, a destruction of the neurons caused by alcohol in the brain's mammillary bodies (a nucleus of cells connected to the hippocampus) while the rest of the brain remains perfectly preserved. The symptoms of this disease curiously resemble accounts of some electroshock patients in which childhood memories are clear while many more recent years of life disappear. These patients, like myself, luckily do not suffer Jimmie G.'s total and irremediable moment-to-moment forgetfulness.

In an epigraph preceding this case study, Oliver Sacks quotes the film director Luis Buñuel's memoirs: "You have to begin to lose your memory, if only in bits and pieces, to realize that memory is what makes our lives. Life without memory is no life at all. . . . Our memory is our coherence, our reason, our feeling, even our action. Without it we are nothing."

Two fascinating Hollywood movies, made almost sixty years apart, explore two different aspects of memory loss: retrograde amnesia—the inability to recall past events—and anterograde amnesia—the inability to form new memories. In *Random Harvest* (1942), based on the novel by James Hilton and directed by Mervyn LeRoy, an English soldier who goes by the name John Smith (Ronald Colman), suffering from amnesia after bein

shocked during World War I, escapes from the mental asylum
where he has been confined and runs into a showgirl played by
Greer Garson, who befriends him. "I've lost my memory," he tells
her. "I don't even know who I am." "Well, I know who you are,"
she replies. "You're somebody awfully nice. What's your name?"
"Smith, it's not my real name. What's yours?" "Paula. Paula
Ridgeway. That's not my real name either." They marry and live
a blissful life of genteel poverty.

Three years later, on a trip to Liverpool, he is hit by a taxi and
again loses his memory, this time of the years of his life with
Paula. But now he discovers he can recall his life before the war
and his previous identity as Sir Charles Rainier, and he returns to
his family business. Paula, who believes her husband, John
Smith, is dead, one day comes across his photograph in a magazine identifying him as an "Industrial Prince of England" and
manages to get herself hired, unrecognized by him, as his dedicated, persevering secretary. Elected a member of Parliament, he
convinces her to contract with him in a loveless marriage of con-
venience, then becomes increasingly fixated on the mystery of
the forgotten three years of his postwar life and the person with
whom he senses he may have spent those years. Lady Rainier,
imagining that he might even fall in love with her, says to him:
"Your capacity for loving, your joy of living, is buried in the little
space of time you forgot." "I still have hope," he tells her. "You
might even have met the woman you once knew and not known
her," she says; "it might even have been me." Of course he ultimately realizes it had been she, and the memory of his entire life
falls into place as they live happily ever after. (Ironically, considering its depiction of a man suffering from amnesia and what we
would now call post-traumatic stress disorder, *Random Harvest*,
one of the most popular films of 1942, was frequently shown to
American soldiers overseas during World War II.)

In *Memento* (2000), directed and written by Christopher
Nolan, the protagonist is an insurance investigator named
Leonard (played by Guy Pearce), who, traumatized by the murder
of his wife, finds himself unable to form new memories after receiving a blow to the head. Suffering from anterograde amnesia —

not short-term memory loss, as Leonard often opines (he doesn't lose memories, he just doesn't form them)—he goes searching for the killer. (The film mirrors his confusion by beginning in the future and moving back to his wife's death.) All the while Leonard is reminding himself of his mission and warning himself about which people to trust and which not to trust by taking and annotating Polaroid photos and by tattooing instructions on his arms and chest: DON'T BELIEVE HIS LIES, DON'T BELIEVE HIM— HE'S THE ONE, FIND HIM AND KILL HIM. ("You really do need a system if you're going to make it work," he says. "You learn to trust your own handwriting.")

Leonard is befriended by a woman (played by Carrie-Anne Moss) named Natalie (NATALIE HAS ALSO LOST SOMEONE/SHE'LL HELP YOU OUT OF PITY), who tells him, "Even if you get revenge, you won't be able to remember it. You're not going to know it happened." Condemned to live only in the fractured present, he struggles on. And through Leonard's haunting voice-overs, the film conveys his experience from the inside and, from the outside, depicts a person whose memories fade at the very moment they are formed, leading to a life of disconnection and loss.

In Gabriel García Márquez's *One Hundred Years of Solitude*, a plague is visited upon the mythical Colombian village of Macondo, resulting in the gradual loss of memory of all the inhabitants. Childhood recollections fade along with the people's awareness of their identities. In order to aid them in remembering, the village patriarch, José Arcadio Buendía, writes down the names of objects: table, chair, clock, door, wall, bed. He also labels the animals: cow, goat, pig, hen. Realizing that, in spite of preserving these names, the Macondians will soon forget the functions of their animals, he decides to hang a sign on the neck of a cow, for example, stating: "This is the cow. She must be milked every morning so that she will produce milk, and the milk must be boiled in order to be mixed with coffee to make coffee and milk." And on the road to the village, he erects a sign that says MACONDO and a larger sign announcing GOD EXISTS.

But José Arcadio soon realizes that the reality and meaning of everything, now captured by words, will vanish when the villagers inevitably forget the meaning of the written letters. He now goes about constructing a memory machine, with which he hopes to record the totality of the villagers' knowledge, and succeeds in gathering 14,000 entries. In the end, a traveler, whom he once knew but no longer recognizes, produces a flask containing a wondrous liquid. When they drink from it, the memories of José Arcadio Buendía and the villagers are magically restored.

For me, the most extraordinary fictional representation of the loss of memory occurs in Nicole Krauss's novel *Man Walks into a Room* (2002), the story of a thirty-six-year-old Columbia University professor of English named Samson Greene, whom the police find wandering disheveled and in a kind of fugue state through the Mojave Desert. Having recently undergone a craniotomy to remove a brain tumor, Samson realizes that he has forgotten twenty-four years of his life. And after being brought back to New York City, he discovers that he can no longer recognize his wife, Anna. He tries to form new memories of this unknown woman, studying her face and body at night as she sleeps next to him, trying to remember her now so that he might recognize her in the morning. But as time passes, Samson discovers that he has less and less desire to have his memory return, choosing instead the freedom and clarity of the moment, emptying himself of the weight of the past in order to create a new life for himself in the future.

Giving up his city, friends, home, and life with Anna, Samson travels back to the Mojave Desert to volunteer for a futuristic memory transfer project. This project is led by a neuroscientist named Ray Malcolm, who dreams of mitigating the terror of man's aloneness in the universe by allowing people to experience one another's consciousness. (It is interesting to note that in the 1960s and '70s a number of fascinating, controversial, and now discredited experiments entailed injecting peptides from one rat's brain into another with results that were thought to suggest the possibility of behavior transfers.) Assisted by a team of neuropsychologists, computer scientists, engineers, and lab technicians, Ray plans to transfer a memory recorded on a computer from an ex-G.I. named Donald Selwyn into Samson's brain. Donald has been selected to donate a specific memory—of an atomic bomb test he witnessed in 1957, while he was serving in the army—a memory consisting of "neural patterns, firing synapses, axon-to-dendrite, distilled into billions of shards of data and stored in gigabytes, a memory of a few moments broken down into billions of binaries, one or zero." Lying in the dark fully wired, the drugs seeping into his bloodstream, his mind loosening its hold on him, Samson has a sudden flash of Anna's face, then falls into a state of confusion that lasts until an explosion blasts everything away.

Later, as Samson wakes to the sound of a countdown and a detonation, he tries to calm himself by imagining this as just one more memory, to be forgotten with all the others, except that this memory ineluctably brings him back to the picture of a decimated Hiroshima he saw on television when he was five years old that haunted his childhood and will now haunt the rest of his life. "Curled on the desert floor under the unjust stars," Krauss writes, "silently weeping for all he had forgotten and could not change, he let himself remember only the things he could. . . . Begin again with nothing, or almost nothing, and still one must begin."

CHAPTER TWO

On Wanting to Forget

A Conversation with James L. McGaugh

> Canst thou not minister to a mind diseased,
> Pluck from the memory a rooted sorrow,
> Raze out the written troubles of the brain,
> And with some sweet oblivious antidote
> Cleanse the stuffed bosom of that perilous stuff
> Which weighs upon the heart?
>
> William Shakespeare,
> *Macbeth*

MARCEL PROUST SPENT HIS LIFE IN SEARCH OF LOST TIME. THE French composer Pierre Boulez, however, proposed the provocative notion that "the strongest civilizations are those without memory—those capable of complete forgetfulness. They are strong enough to destroy because they know they can replace what is destroyed." (Think of the Renaissance, however, when it was said that "one moves forward by looking back.") Many persons today fantasize about the possibility of wiping out discomforting memories in order to live more happily in the present. As one of my friends told me, "I wound up talking to my husband about what memories we would willingly have erased. The main ones I came up with were my memories of a really lame affair I had with this guy from when I lived in Atlanta, and memories of all the times over the years that my mother was ever angry with me." But as a person who has lost many years of his memory, I find doing away with unpleasant remembrances, which we are all heir to—as do the unhappy ex-lovers in the film *Eternal Sunshine of the Spotless Mind*—a peculiar proposition. "When we reflect on the tragedies of our own lives," Thomas Moore remarks in *Care of the Soul,* "when we slowly find our way through their miseries, we are being initiated into the mysterious ways of the soul. Love is the means of entry and our guide." So why desire to erase these memories? "Memory," as Saul Bellow writes, "is life."

Any attempt to attenuate the effects of post-traumatic stress disorder, by contrast, is obviously an urgent and humane undertaking to save people from unmitigated nightmares and paralyzing flashbacks resulting from memories of combat atrocities, car crashes, or sexual assaults. It has been estimated that 10 to 15 percent of persons who have experienced such traumas develop post-traumatic stress disorder.

Our remembrance of experiences tends to vary directly with their emotional significance. What has been called "motivated forgetting" can often alleviate less stressful memories. A team of researchers from the University of Oregon have found that unwanted memories can be driven from awareness. They have identified a brain circuit that is activated when people deliberately try to forget something, suggesting a neurological basis for how we can bury painful memories in the subconscious. It has been demonstrated, for example, that persons who deliberately attempt to keep a word out of their minds find it more difficult to recall the word later than if they had not suppressed it.

But for those who do suffer from post-traumatic stress disorder, the groundbreaking work of the neurobiologist James L. McGaugh has given hope for relief. In the mid-1990s, McGaugh, in collaboration with the neurobiologist Larry Cahill, made the important discovery that one could impede the development of the "black hole" memories of this disorder by using beta-blockers such as propranolol to block the action of stress hormones like adrenaline and noradrenaline. This discovery has led to promising therapeutic attempts by the biological psychiatrist Roger Pitman of Harvard University to use propranolol in treatment for post-traumatic stress disorder.

James L. McGaugh is director of the Center for the Neurobiology of Learning and Memory and professor of neurobiology

and behavior at the University of California, Irvine. He is the author of textbooks on neuroscience and psychology and of *Memory
and Emotion: The Making of Lasting Memories,* an illuminating,
compendious, and accessible work based on state-of-the-art scientific research. (McGaugh says this book was intended to be a
"conversation with my reader.")

James L. McGaugh spoke to me from his office at the University of California, Irvine.

In Memory and Emotion, *you write: "Memories are generally good
things to have. Our records of our personal past are essential in enabling us to survive. All of our knowledge of our world, and our
skills in living in it, are based on memories of our experiences. So,
too, are all of our plans and dreams. Life without memory is difficult to imagine." Why the "generally"?*

What I mean by that is that some memories are bad to have. I was
on a talk show the other day in Los Angeles, and they asked me
about the ethics of using a drug to block the development of post-
traumatic stress disorder [PTSD]. I'm not doing PTSD research,
but others are doing it based, at least partly, on the work I have
done. And I said, Why don't you ask people who have PTSD if
they would like not to have it? And immediately we got a phone
call in from a man who said, in very terse terms, "In September of
1999 both of my children were killed in an automobile accident.
If there had been a pill to prevent the horror I'm now going
through, I would have taken two." That's what I mean when I say
memories are *generally* good things to have. Memories can nag
us, haunt us, and at the extreme, prevent us from functioning effectively.

*You've also said that selectivity in creating memories is critically
important; that most of our trivial experiences are, and should be,
forgettable; and that for most of us, built-in neurobiological systems automatically provide that needed selectivity. Could you say
something about how these neurological systems work?*

Let's start with the premise that it's a good thing to have selectivity in memory. What I mean by that is that if you remembered everything equally well, using your recollected memories would be like searching in a junkyard trying to find things that you're interested in but can't find because there are too many things to consider—causing confusion. So what we need to have is a memory that will allow us to remember selectively: "Oh, yes, it was today that I parked my car *there*, not to be confused with where I parked it three weeks ago last Wednesday." We need that selectivity.

Now, how does this work? There's substantial evidence that emotionally significant experiences are better remembered. Such experiences consist of horrific experiences, such as those of a woman who e-mailed me yesterday. Her son was missing, and she went out into the woods to look for him . . . and she found him: he'd taken his father's shotgun and blown most of his head off. She said, "Can you get rid of this picture in my mind?" Unfortunately, she'll never forget that. At the other extreme would be somebody who simply gives you a pat on the head or says, "That was a good job," or "Congratulations," or "I love you," or something like that. That's not like seeing your son who has had his face and his head blown off. But these are all emotional experiences, and they're going to be better remembered.

Now what happens is that even the slightest emotional experience, such as a "congratulations" or some embarrassing gaffe that you have made, will release stress hormones—cortisol and adrenaline—from the adrenal glands. These stress hormones are released by any mildly or extremely emotionally arousing event, and they can directly and indirectly influence brain activity. In particular, they influence a very important part of the brain called the amygdala, which is located in the middle part of the temporal lobes. They activate the release of noradrenaline in the amygdala, and that turns out to be a key event underlying the influence of emotional arousal on subsequent long-term memory. If drugs that block the action of the noradrenaline are infused into this region of the brains of laboratory animals, they will block the effects of emotional arousal on memory.

The next stage is the activation of the neural pathways that go to other regions of the brain where the memories are being processed. Such influences instruct the other regions of the brain to make stronger neural changes that begin the process of consolidating memory. Thus, as you have an experience, memory processing starts in lots of different brain regions. To the extent that that experience is exciting, it causes release of adrenaline and cortisol, which also then act on the amygdala, and the amygdala being activated then amplifies the neural changes that are taking place in other regions of the brain to create a stronger memory.

To make this concrete, in Memory and Emotion *you describe a scene in medieval times, before writing was used to keep historical records, when means other than writing had to be found to maintain records of important events such as a wedding or negotiations between powerful families. You say that a child about seven years old was selected, instructed to observe the proceedings carefully, and then thrown into a river. In this way, it was said, the memory of the event would be impressed on the child and the record of the event maintained for the child's lifetime. That hyperactive amygdala was certainly working overtime.*

That's right. This example is from medieval lore, but a classics scholar told me that it has its origins in Greek history. So apparently this is something that's been known for thousands of years, and I just happened to pick up a medieval version of it. But it certainly makes the point.

In the mid-1990s you and Larry Cahill discovered that one could use beta-blockers like propranolol to block the action of stress hormones, thus attenuating the effects of the development of PTSD as a result of things like combat atrocities or car crashes. What led to this discovery?

What led us to that discovery was several prior decades of research in my laboratory investigating the effects of drugs administered to animals immediately after they had been trained on some task. We found that we could enhance memory by administering many kinds of drugs, including adrenaline and drugs that mimic the actions of adrenaline, and we could block memory formation by giving drugs that blocked the action of adrenaline. Propranolol is one of the class of beta-blockers that do the latter. We demonstrated that we could do that either when the drugs were administered into the body systemically (that is, subcutaneously) or when the drugs were injected directly into the amygdala.

So, on the basis of these animal experiments, Larry Cahill and I decided to investigate whether a beta-blocker administered to human subjects would prevent the enhancing effect of emotional arousal on memory. Thus, the Cahill study is a direct extension of experiments we had already done with laboratory animals. That's how we happened to do it—we knew that it worked in animals, so we could ask the same experimental question in human subjects. And the answer was clear: the beta-blocker was effective in preventing the memory enhancement induced by emotional arousal. Our findings have been replicated in several subsequent studies.

And I know that this became a benchmark study. How is propranolol being used therapeutically today?

Its major use is in the treatment of heart disease. It's used by millions of people. And not only propranolol but other beta-blockers as well. What they do is sit on cells and prevent the action of noradrenaline and adrenaline.

A friend told me that he had taken propranolol in order to mitigate his phobia of public speaking and stage fright.

That's a secondary use which is rather extensive. Many if not most students of music and drama know about propranolol. When they get to a biology class, they already know about it because they've been taking it to aid their performances.

Isn't the primary focus of research today on its possible efficacy with regard to memory erasure?

That is *a* focus of research that grew out of the work Larry Cahill did with me. Here's what happened. Dr. Roger Pitman at Harvard University read our research findings and called me up one day to say he wanted to talk with me. The next day he was in my office. And what he said was that our research findings were relevant to his thinking about the development of PTSD. He suggested that PTSD resulting from a traumatic experience develops as a consequence of frequent inadvertent rehearsal of that experience *after* the experience. So let's say someone is assaulted. The next day the remembrance of the assault flashes into his or her mind along with emotional arousal. It's this inadvertent rehearsal over a period of several weeks that Pitman believes is at least partly responsible for the development of PTSD. My research with Cahill fits in very nicely with this view, because it is possible that with each of these inadvertent rehearsals an emotional response may boost the strength of the memory such that over time the inadvertent rehearsal leads to a very strong memory that can provide the basis for the symptoms of PTSD.

To investigate this idea, Pitman decided to give propranolol, which we had used in our experimental studies, to human subjects quickly after they'd been assaulted, to maintain them on the drug for ten days to two weeks, and then to test them a couple of months later for the signs of PTSD. And in his first study the results were clear: propranolol-treated subjects had reduced signs of PTSD. His finding was replicated by a French group in 2003. So we now have two studies demonstrating that treatment with a beta-blocker for a two-week period after a trauma appears to attenuate the intensity of the PTSD assessed a couple of months later.

Does propranolol simply mitigate the pain of traumatic memories or actually erase them?

It mitigates, it does not erase. What it does is make memories less intense. I get e-mails every day about this. The woman who sent me the e-mail about her son's head being blown off said, Please help me erase that picture in my mind. That's what she wants to have done. I have several other e-mails like that. People have these horrible memories and would like to get rid of them. But if they're old memories, that's not going to happen. If it's a new memory in the process of being formed, then it can be prevented from being formed. Think of it this way: The person who has been assaulted is going to remember the assault, but the strength of that memory isn't going to be increased with every repetition if they are under the influence of a beta-blocker.

In Philip K. Dick's science-fiction story "Paycheck," which was made into a movie, a reverse engineer enables companies to steal and improve the technology of their rivals, then has the memory of his accomplishment erased by having individual neurons zapped. Do you think targeted memory erasures will be possible in the future?

No. Mainly because the best guess is that memory circuits, to the extent that there are such circuits in the brain, are widely distributed. So how would you be able to find a very specific circuit if one indeed exists? Furthermore, every circuit we have of memory is going to be deeply embedded with others, so I don't see them as existing in isolation. Suppose that it was important for you to forget about automobiles: you have a notion of a general automobile, you also know about a particular automobile, you've had many experiences in automobiles. Automobiles are embedded in memories of different kinds of things; you've taken trips in automobiles, and so on. Now how in the world could I ever go into your brain and pull out whatever it is that consists of "automobile" without damaging all the rest of that?

Second, if I ask you to remember something, that's a constructive process. And we don't believe that a specific memory is located in a very specific place in the brain. Why? Because when you recall something, you have to pull out all the information that's in your brain that will enable you to make the utterance of, in this case, "automobile." Suppose I ask you to imagine something that's shaped in a rectangle and it's got a wheel on each corner and then toward the front of it is a rod that sticks up and it has a wheel on it. And then there is a gasoline engine that's just in front of that between the two front wheels. You've got that? I'm beginning to construct for you an automobile. Now, when I ask you to think of an automobile, you have to draw out of your brain all of the elements that will construct "automobile" as opposed to constructing "bicycle." Just find that and pull it together, and that becomes your memory at that time of an automobile.

So the word *remembering* is quite an appropriate term—put a hyphen between the *re* and the *membering*. Putting the members back together is what remembering is. It's not like fishing, where there's a fish down there and you're going to put a hook on the line and bring up the fish. It's as though there are no fishes in there and you put something in there that reconstructs the fish. The different elements of the memory are there, but when you reconstruct, when you re-member, you bring it together and you create a memory. So those are two reasons why I think it will never be possible selectively to destroy a single memory.

Now, there's another way to destroy memory, and that is anything that's just created—only a new memory—can be abolished for a short period of time. It's very fragile, and certain conditions will lead to that memory not being permanently formed. And I go into that in considerable detail in *Memory and Emotion: The Making of Lasting Memories.*

I had a large number of ECT treatments, and though I am aware that among scientists and doctors there are arguments about whether ECT can permanently erase memories, from my own experience—and the testimonies of scores of other persons who have experienced the same problem—I can say that many years of my memories have entirely disappeared, though I know, of course, that this hasn't been the case with everybody who has had ECT treatments.

In the 1880s a French psychologist named Théodule Ribot studied the effects of brain injury on memory. He discovered that when the brain was injured, the most recently acquired memories were lost and the older memories were preserved. So the effect was like a labor union or personnel policy—last in, first fired. That memory effect has been found with patients who have had ECT, with retrograde amnesia extending back at least two or three years. Larry Squire, at the University of California at San Diego, has published such findings. The important question is not whether there is retrograde amnesia induced by ECT but whether the memory loss is permanent or only temporary. That is, is there any recovery of those lost memories over time even if there's evidence of retrograde amnesia shortly after the treatment? Considerable evidence suggests that amnesia for experiences occurring just prior to and after ECT treatment is permanent.

As I said, I've permanently lost many years of my memory.

That would be unusual for ECT to have such an effect, although there are examples from studies of brain injury where retrograde amnesia has been reported to extend for a period of several years. We don't have a ready explanation for extended retrograde amnesia other than to say it looks as though such memories are consolidated over a very long period of time.

My childhood memories and those for most of my life are pretty good.

And that's consistent with the general conclusion suggested by considerable evidence from clinical studies of memory. However, it would be unusual for ECT to induce a long-term memory loss of the kind you apparently have.

Aside from ECT and propranolol, are there any other drugs that can erase memories? Years ago I was prescribed Halcion and Ativan, and I couldn't remember a thing that happened to me during the time I was on those medications.

Yes, such drugs can prevent memories from being stored. They don't have a retrograde amnesia effect, but if you take a healthy dose of one of those drugs (or any of the benzodiazepine drugs), you may appear to be learning and performing perfectly normally and yet you may not effectively store the information that you're acquiring while you're under the influence of the drugs. Those drugs induce anterograde amnesia—that is, they prevent the storage of something you've learned after you've taken the drug. But as soon as the drug effects wear off, your learning and memory return to normal.

When I took them it was like a lost weekend!

[Laughing] When the drugs came out, they were prescribed for anxiety, and then psychiatrists began to get the reports back from patients saying things such as "I just returned from a business trip and I don't remember much of what happened on that trip." Later on there were studies of that phenomenon, and finally the U.K. banned Halcion. However, unlike ECT, benzodiazepines don't induce retrograde amnesia.

In the film Eternal Sunshine of the Spotless Mind, *two unhappy ex-lovers visit a lab to have neurotechnicians attempt to erase their memories of each other. Why do you think a film like this and a story (and film) like "Paycheck" reverberate so strongly in people's imaginations today? Why are people so fascinated with the possibility of erasing memories, especially at a time when millions of people are suffering from Alzheimer's disease?*

I can only speculate on that. But the question helps explain why I am so interested in understanding memory. We have this magical machine in our heads that captures the experiences we have and retains them. So what we've got, if you like, is a rearview mirror on life; we can look in our rearview mirror and see where we've been. It's really a magic show. You can close your eyes right now and remember when you dialed me on the phone to have this conversation, you can remember what you did earlier today, and you may have thought earlier today that you had to remember to call me at a certain time . . . and all of it's there. What on earth is that all about? How do we carry this machine in our heads? We can call up these magic events in our heads, and we can rearrange them in ways that will lead to planning. How do we do that? So I think that's part of the fascination—the fact that we carry around with us not only our present experiences but records of our past experiences as well. Magic. Magic. Magic.

Now, when we recall memories that we don't want to have, it can be disturbing. I've had people say to me, "I want to forget my ex-spouse; I don't want to remember him or her anymore. I'd like to put those memories away in a storage closet and leave them there. But I remember them again and again. How can I get rid of those memories?" For more intense memories, consider the woman who said, "I'd like to forget that I found my son with his head blown off." Our musing about memory ranges all the way from the fascination of just thinking about our memories to the reality of having awful memories that we'd like to get rid of. I said that memories are generally a good thing to have. Not always.

The New York Times *did a Web Pulse survey which asked whether people would use memory blockers, and the results were that 29 percent would use them and 71 percent would not.*

In considering those percentages, it is worth noting that of the people who have traumatic experiences, only about 15 percent, on average, will have any signs of PTSD. And of those, perhaps only a few are disabled by the memories. So it's not a problem for most people. To me that 29 percent of people who would use memory blockers seems very high. It's a bit troublesome that almost 30 percent of the population feel that they have memories they would like to get rid of.

Does that surprise you?

Yes. But such memories may differ considerably among individuals. For example, some people might like to forget an embarrassing event, a failed job interview, or a nasty interchange with someone at the office. Soldiers might want to forget seeing their friends' heads getting blown off. Those are, of course, very different kinds of bad memories.

There's a spiritual idea that's widely held about living in the present, in the moment, like water down a brook or wind across the desert. For many people this is a longed-for state. But is the wish to erase memories in order to achieve such a state desirable or even possible?

First of all, it's impossible. Let me back up a little bit. The truth is that each of our lives is only a half a second long anyway. Because by the time a half a second goes by, it's already in memory. Right? I said "Right" then, but as soon as I said it, it's a memory, it's not there. So the truth is that in fact we're only in the present. However, that present exists only because of memory. You look around your room, maybe there's a lamp there.

I'm looking at it now.

You know what that is, don't you? You're not startled when you look at it. You're living in the present and you're seeing the lamp, but you know what that is; that means your memory allows you to do that. You're talking on a telephone, you're not saying, What on earth is this? Even to do that you're using memory, because you're using language that you have learned. It would be impossible for you to exist without your memories; you could make no sense of who or where you are. So even though you're only capturing a glimpse of the world half a second at a time, the fact that you're able to make that glimpse is substantially dependent on the memories you already have. Your existence today is enabled by your memories. So if you were to create a situation in which you were devoid of your past, you would have no present. Experience the present without a past? Impossible. I think it's a logical impossibility and nonsense as well.

"Memory," you write in Memory and Emotion, *"in a most general sense is the lasting consequence of an experience. . . . Our lives require that we record our experiences." How does one learn from experience and understand and examine one's past and grow and change and, as you say, react appropriately to changing experiences if one erases one's memories? Take the couple in* Eternal Sunshine of the Spotless Mind. *After having their memories of each other erased, they meet up again as if for the first time, and one wonders whether they won't make the same mistakes with each other that they did before and won't want to have their memories of each other erased once again!*

If you totally erase your memories and prevent the formation of new memories, then you prevent growth, you prevent change. There are plenty of human patients around who have lost that ability by virtue of having damage to the brain. They are permanently frozen at one particular point in time and can't benefit from their experiences. There are people who have damage to the medial temporal lobes who can no longer learn any new explicit knowledge about the world. These patients live in the present on the basis of memories that they've already acquired, but they can't acquire new information about the world, so they have to be taken care of.

William Faulkner wrote that between grief and nothing, he would take grief. Since memories are who we are, aren't painful ones also part of who we are?

Painful ones are part of who we are, it's a question of who you want to be. However, if you have extraordinarily painful memories, you can imagine that you'd rather not have them. Just as if you have a sore foot, you'd like to get it healed. If you have terrible memories disrupting your life, you may well want to get rid of those memories. That's why those people are sending me e-mails describing horrific memories. Yes, their memories are part of their lives, but it doesn't mean that they are good parts of their lives.

CHAPTER THREE

On Alzheimer's Disease

A Conversation with David Shenk

Just as the child loses, as he comes into the world,
his angelic memory, so the man, as he grows old,
loses his memory of this world.

Bronson Alcott,
quoted by Ralph Waldo Emerson

In order to be yourself, you have to remember who you
were and are. Alzheimer's disease is the ultimate manifestation of
forgetting, the gradual unraveling of mind, soul, and body, a life
without identity and awareness. As a sufferer in the earlier stages
of the disease recounts: "The other day I was all confused in the
street for a split second. I had to ask somebody where I was, and I
realized that this is a whole structure in which a window falls out,
and then suddenly before you know it, the whole facade breaks
apart. This is the worst thing that can happen to a thinking person. You can feel yourself, your whole inside and outside, break
down."

More than 5 million Americans and perhaps 15 million people worldwide suffer from Alzheimer's disease. By 2050, as the
population increasingly ages, about 15 million people in the
United States alone will have Alzheimer's, at an annual cost of as
much as $700 billion. "Why are so many people fascinated by
Alzheimer's disease?" asks David Shenk in his illuminating book
The Forgetting: Alzheimer's: Portrait of an Epidemic. "Because,"
he writes, "it is not only a disease, but also a prism through which
we can view life in ways not normally available to us. . . . It is

more painful than many people can even imagine, but it is also perhaps the most poignant of all reminders of why and how human life is so extraordinary. It is our best lens on the meaning of loss."

Shenk, the author of *Data Smog: Surviving the Information Glut*, came to the writing of his book on Alzheimer's because of a woman he never met, whose name he never knew. Eating lunch alone one day in his neighborhood taqueria, he found himself absorbed by a nearby conversation about this woman with early-onset Alzheimer's who could no longer recognize her own husband. "I closed my eyes," Shenk recalls, "and tried to imagine myself as that husband, and then stumbled back to my office determined to learn more about this disease." *The Forgetting* is a profound and beautifully written work that explores the worlds of literature, art, history, genetics, and neurobiology as it reveals and sheds light on the mysteries of the forgetting mind.

I spoke with David Shenk at his home in Brooklyn, New York.

Can you say something about the neuropathologist Alois Alzheimer and about the date November 25, 1901, when a fifty-one-year-old woman was admitted to the psychiatric hospital in Frankfurt, Germany?

Without Dr. Alzheimer, of course, we wouldn't have the name Alzheimer's associated with this disease, which is a strange thought because it's so fittingly haunting. It's called Alzheimer's because Alois Alzheimer happened to be the right man in the right place at the right time and had just the right level of curiosity. He was the attending physician on that day in 1901 when a woman whom we know as Auguste D. was brought in by her husband. She was displaying what we would now call classic signs of the early stages of Alzheimer's disease—a very debilitated short-term memory, some paranoid fantasies, and she was making all kinds of mistakes in the kitchen, she wasn't able to remember where she had left things. Today, these are all classic symptoms of Alzheimer's. And yet to Alois Alzheimer in 1901, it was unusual.

Senile dementia is something that every culture has been fa-

miliar with, going back to the beginning of recorded history. The
observation that some people who get very old begin to lose their
memories has been around forever. And up until recently, that's
been accepted as just a part of life. Senile dementia wasn't considered a disease.

But Auguste D. was relatively young, and that caught Dr.
Alzheimer's attention. He spoke her full name and asked her to
write it down. She couldn't do it. From the moment of hearing
her name to the two or three seconds later of trying to write it
down with a pencil—that simple piece of memory she could not
preserve. She kept writing pieces of the name. Finally, at the third
or fourth prompting, she was able to write out her full first name
and the initial D. She put her pencil down and said, "I have lost
myself." I came upon that statement fairly early on in my research, and I was just blown away. I somehow knew right then
that I wouldn't come upon a more poignant summary for what
this disease is: losing one's self. It's people not dying physically
but watching their own cognition, their own awareness of themselves and of everything else, fade away—and fade away so slowly
that for a while they're actually able to *see* it fade away. That is really the seminal horror of Alzheimer's disease, the idea that a person is eroding from the inside, becoming an empty shell.

No one wants to die, or to have one's loved ones die—so it's
odd to contemplate that there are better and worse ways of dying.
But there are. And when you are forced to think about it, you realize that if you *could* choose, for yourself or for the people you
care about, you would definitely choose an instant death over a
slow fade. The best way to go is just to keel over one day and that's
that. No one wants to face the physical pain of cancer or other de-
generative diseases. But Alzheimer's is arguably the worst, because it's the slowest. There's no physical pain, but the torment
endured by friends and family over those ten or so years is just ex-
cruciating.

Getting back to how the disease was named: Dr. Alzheimer realized that his patient Auguste D. had some form of dementia,
but it obviously wasn't senile dementia because she wasn't elderly. So he was very curious about her and followed her closely

and wanted to look inside her brain. As both a clinician and a pathologist, he was able to view her condition from both sides of the fence. When she died five years later, he immediately sent for some of her brain tissue and saw for himself the plaques and tangles—the two markers of the disease. They proved that she had had an organic brain disease, not some sort of mental imbalance. He could see with his own eyes the deterioration of the brain tissue. It was a pioneering moment in neurology.

When did Alzheimer's disease become Alzheimer's disease?

The term was introduced in 1910—but with a very restricted meaning. From 1910 until the 1970s, "Alzheimer's disease" was used to denote those who succumbed to senile dementia in their forties, fifties, and early sixties—what we now call "early-onset Alzheimer's." The elderly senile weren't considered to have a disease at all—they were just getting this normal, if regrettable, condition. And to this day, many doctors educated in that period still use the term Alzheimer's only to refer to these early-onset patients.

So before the 1970s, Alzheimer's was considered a very rare disorder. But what doctors finally realized about thirty years ago is that there is no real difference in the pathology of the disease whether you get it when you're fifty or seventy-five or ninety. Whatever the age, it's still those plaques and tangles slowly creeping into your brain. They start in the hippocampus and then very slowly work their way through the rest of the brain, destroying neurons as they go along.

Plaques float between the neurons, and long, black, stringy tangles choke neurons from inside their cell membranes, and it seems as if plaques and tangles are the two bogeymen of Alzheimer's disease.

That's right. Probably just one of them alone would be enough to do some serious damage. Together, it seems to be kind of a one-two punch. But to this day, scientists don't quite understand the relationship between the two, or their relative destructive power.

Does one cause the other? Does one do more damage than the other? If there's any serious conflict in Alzheimer's research right now, it's between the people who believe that it's more important to pay attention to the tangles—a small minority—and the rest, perhaps 75 percent, who believe it's more important to pay attention to the plaques, the big round globules outside the neurons. Most of the drug development right now is aimed at removing the plaques, or preventing their formation, because most people believe that if they can take care of the plaques they can take care of the disease.

You write, "Alzheimer's overtakes a person very gradually and for a while can be indistinguishable from mild memory loss." The first few slips may perhaps seem the result of momentary confusion, absentmindedness, or anxiety, but then the isolated incidents start to mount. Can you describe some of the incipient symptoms of Alzheimer's and the early signs of what you call the "long fade" and what the neuroscientist Joseph LeDoux calls "cognitive meltdown"?

It's common to have memory lapses. Everyone has them—I'm thirty-six and I have them all the time. They are particularly common to people who are middle-aged or older. Part of it is biological—you are getting older and a little slower—but it's also cultural: you're getting older, you're dealing with more things in your life, you have more to remember, you have more responsibilities, more things that you're interested in. There's a tremendous rise in expectations as you get into your thirties and beyond. You want to keep learning new things but also retain everything you've come into contact with—all the people, all the ideas, all the things you've read. So people are inherently disappointed with their memories as they get older.

The difference between normal memory trouble and Alzheimer's is imperceptible at the very beginning of the disease. But then, slowly, things start to get worse. There are little moments of confusion. The person is driving home and is making the same turn onto a street that he's made fifteen hundred times. But just for a moment he doesn't know where he is. Just for a split second—then right back to normal.

That happened to Ronald Reagan pretty early on. It was about six years after the end of his presidency, and he was visiting Washington for what turned out to be the last time. He gave a speech and delivered it beautifully, but then back at the hotel he was going up to his room and he stopped for a second and said, "Well, I've got to stop, I just don't know where I am right now." That was a sign that he might be in the very early stages.

From the patients' point of view, it may not look like there's a problem at all. They're not aware that they are forgetting. The memory isn't being lost per se—it was never actually formed.

I've heard that denial of one's early symptoms is an important part of the Alzheimer's experience.

Quite often, but it's not universal. There are some people who are comfortable in looking closely at themselves and wanting to confront any little issue that's going on in their lives, and those people embrace the truth right away—not happily, but they do face it. More often, though, it's just an overwhelming concept that you are losing hold of your brain, and denial is one of the great lifesaving psychological mechanisms that we have. If we didn't have it, we'd all go bonkers whenever something horrible happened to us. Denial is just something we need at certain points in our lives.

Could you describe some of the symptoms of the middle and late stages of Alzheimer's?

Broadly outlined, the signs of the early stages would be short-term memory disorder, a little bit of confusion, sometimes some paranoia, but for the most part people look and feel like themselves. When they get to the middle stage of the disease, which generally speaking is a couple of years later, they will be confused all the time. Their short-term memory will be obliterated—they won't be remembering anything from one moment to the next. They'll need twenty-four-hour care. They can't take care of themselves anymore—whereas in the early stages people can make Post-it notes to themselves and pretty much live on their own if they have to. By the middle stage that's not the case.

But physically people are still very much intact. There may be a little bit of imbalance, a little bit of hesitancy in their walking around. But to other people—and this is really striking—you can meet middle-stage Alzheimer's people and they're still talking, they have the same cadence to their voices, and if you don't sit there for a number of minutes and really pay attention to what they're saying and realize that some of it is utter nonsense, you can feel and think that you're having a very normal conversation with a person who's entirely healthy. This is very strange for outsiders, and I've experienced this many times: only when you go home do you reflect on that conversation and realize that it really didn't make sense.

In the late stages of Alzheimer's disease, people are utterly gone cognitively and they're starting to deteriorate physically. This happens in stages: first they won't be able to walk as well as they once did, then they won't be able to walk at all, eventually they won't be able to sit up, and finally they start to lose all control over their muscles. And for the people who live long enough, live to the very end and don't die of something else first, their control of their basic life support functions, like swallowing and breathing, is eventually snuffed out. A lot of Alzheimer's patients never get to those end stages—they die of something else along the way. They get cancer or suffer a heart attack and die. But a number of people do make it to the very end, and the disease will eventually kill you.

In your book you talk about the New York University neurologist Barry Reisberg and his amazing analogy between Alzheimer's and childhood development, suggesting that there is a precise inverse relationship between stages of Alzheimer's and phases of child development in the areas of cognition, language, feeding, and behavior. As you point out, Alzheimer's unravels the brain almost exactly in the reverse order as it develops from birth, revealing a kind of reverse childhood in a process that Reisberg terms "retrogenesis."

Reisberg documents these observations in comparison charts; and placed side by side, the sequences of abilities gained and lost almost perfectly mirror one another. (I am reproducing these comparison charts here as Shenk paraphrases them in his book.)

CHILD DEVELOPMENT

AGE	ACQUIRED ABILITY
1–3 months	Can hold up head
2–4 months	Can smile
6–10 months	Can sit up without assistance
1 year	Can walk without assistance
1 year	Can speak one word
15 months	Can speak five to six words
2–3 years	Can control bowels
3–4.5 years	Can control urine
4 years	Can use toilet without assistance
4–5 years	Can adjust bath water temperature
4–5 years	Can put on clothes without assistance
5–7 years	Can select proper clothing for occasion or season
8–12 years	Can handle simple finances
12+ years	Can hold a job, prepare meals, etc.

ALZHEIMER'S DISEASE

STAGE	LOST ABILITY
1	No difficulty at all
2	Some memory trouble begins to affect job/home
3	Much difficulty maintaining job performance
4	Can no longer hold a job, prepare meals, handle personal finances, etc.
5	Can no longer select proper clothing for occasion or season
6a	Can no longer put on clothes properly
6b	Can no longer adjust bath water temperature
6c	Can no longer use toilet without assistance

6d	Urinary incontinence
6e	Fecal incontinence
7a	Speech now limited to six or so words per day
7b	Speech now limited to one word per day
7c	Can no longer walk without assistance
7d	Can no longer sit up without assistance
7e	Can no longer smile
7f	Can no longer hold up head

Many Alzheimer's caregivers have raised children at some point in their lives, and the comparisons are unavoidable. It can often feel like taking care of a child in reverse. It starts out that you're dealing with someone who is fully mature, has lived a presumably healthy, self-sustaining life, and all of a sudden needs just a little bit of help, the way a ten-year-old might. And then very slowly, as the Alzheimer's patients start to lose abilities, they need more and more help, as if they were ten-year-olds getting younger and younger.

This is a concept that you find throughout literature. Shakespeare wrote about "second childishness," and there are ancient Greek writers who compare senile dementia to the behavioral abilities of young children. So what Barry Reisberg did was to point out that his comparison charts might be useful in order to enable caregivers to prepare emotionally and physically for what's ahead of them. I mean, the nice thing about raising two-year-olds is that they're going to get older and less dependent on you, and if you have any question about what's coming your way, about any trouble or any new problems, you can just ask someone who's got a two-year-old. So Reisberg had the idea that we can do the same thing for Alzheimer's caregivers, as if to say, "This is a disease that moves, it changes, it's a very different disease from year to year because of its progression, so let's prepare a little bit for what's going to happen."

Right now you've got someone who can't form new memories, but basically he's okay. Well, in a year or two, here are the things you are going to be dealing with, and in a year or two after that here's what you'll be dealing with. And Reisberg realized that for people who have taken care of children already, putting these two lists side by side could be very useful. You have an early-stage Alzheimer's patient who has the abilities of, let's say, a ten-year-old, and in a couple of years he'll act more like an eight-year-old, a couple of more years like a six-year-old, and here's how the abilities will match up. This is not to say that this is a perfect match, but generally here's what you're going to be dealing with and here's how you can think about preparing for it. You've heard of childproofing your home? Well, you have to proof your home for Alzheimer's patients, too, once they get to a certain stage, so that they won't wander out or do things that are a danger to themselves or others.

You say that the notion of reverse childhood turns out to be the best map we have to understand the terrain of Alzheimer's.

What I mean by *terrain* is the course of the disease, where it's going, from point A to point B to point C. Your husband has just been diagnosed with Alzheimer's disease. What does that mean to you—to the map of your life over the next five, ten, fifteen years? The reason this is such a touchy subject is that it is inherently insulting to think about your seventy-year-old husband as a child. The concept, while useful, is a tough pill to swallow. The patient is *not* a child, he's not just beginning life and gaining new abilities. He's a person who's lived a full life and done important things—maybe he's solved important scientific questions himself or written important books or been a senator—

Or a president.

Or a president.

It's said that Reagan eventually got to the point where he had no idea that he had been the president.

But this idea of reverse childhood is a difficult notion for people emotionally to accept, and I tried to write it into the book in such a way that people won't be insulted by it. It's tough enough to lose your loved ones, and you don't want to have people coming along and saying, "Well, they're really not adults anymore, they're children."

There are also analogies between caregivers raising kids and kids becoming caregivers—a kind of reverse parenthood. In a recent memoir about her relationship with her Alzheimer's-suffering father (The House on Beartown Road), *Elizabeth Cohen writes, "Daddy walks around . . . dropping pieces of language behind him, the baby following, picking them up."*

That's a nice line. The daughter becoming the mother is an extremely common phenomenon in Alzheimer's. The people I hear back from are overwhelmingly middle-aged women who are now caregivers. They are raising kids themselves or have often just sent their kids off to college and should now be in the prime of their lives with time to travel—but are instead confronted with a whole new parenting responsibility. They're now having to take care of their father or mother who's in an early stage of Alzheimer's. And that's quite commonly a ten-year burden. But it's not just a burden. It's also a privilege to be close to your parents and to help them, though Alzheimer's caregiving is not anything that anyone plans for or would wish upon themselves.

In your book you talk about the difference between explicit memory, which you call "mind memory" and which deals with the way we know, and implicit memory, which you call "muscle memory" and which deals with the way we act, and it's interesting that in Alzheimer's, mind memory can disappear but muscle memory can still exist, like one's being in a coma while the heart is still beating. And you give an example of the man who cannot recognize his wife but who can still walk or sing or dance a waltz.

Those are two entirely separate systems. I spent some time at a Christmas party for an Alzheimer's group—there were people there with the early stage going on to the middle stage, and they were having a rough time remembering really basic things and were very halting in their speech. But when the music started, they got up and danced these gorgeous waltzes just effortlessly and smoothly.

To be grim about it, you could say it was the last waltz.

That's a nice way of putting it. In fact, those physical abilities do stay intact throughout much of the disease. For a long time you have this very odd dichotomy, such that the patients are losing their cognitions but are very much in control of their muscle movements.

In his book Poetry and Truth, *Goethe tells the story of a French captain who was obsessed by a single idea—that all virtue in the world sprang from a good memory and all vice from forgetfulness. Similarly, in your book you quote Ralph Waldo Emerson (who also had Alzheimer's) as saying, "We estimate a man by how much he remembers." Yet as you point out, Alzheimer's is simply an organic disease in which your brain is under attack, and this doesn't carry any judgmental freight with it; so how do we try to get over the prejudice that forgetting is an example of some kind of moral turpitude?*

What a terrific question. One way to answer it is to talk about the taboo that surrounds Alzheimer's disease and the notion that we need to be afraid of and keep our distance from Alzheimer's patients. For people who talk or write about Alzheimer's, there are two important things to do. One is to educate caregivers as to what they're going through, because it's an incredibly complex disease. It's just very hard to understand—even spending a lot of time with an Alzheimer's patient, you don't intuitively pick up on all of its facets. So in my book I was trying to help caregivers know what they would be going through a little better.

But the other mission, nearly as important, is to help the people outside the world of Alzheimer's, those who haven't yet dealt with the disease, to understand what is going on. We need to break through their ignorance and thereby break through their fear. It's so common for friends and neighbors to avoid people once they have Alzheimer's. As an outsider, you don't understand it and you just want to stay away from it. There're still a lot of people who think you can *catch* Alzheimer's disease, that it's contagious. So on that basic level we have to educate the public. But more than that, people need to understand the contours of the disease, and the stages, so they won't run away. I really want us as a culture to break through that, to understand what Alzheimer's patients are going through and to be able to help each other.

What do you think might be a possible amelioration and ultimately a possible cure for the disease?

I'm incredibly optimistic about this. I got to know a lot of scientists, who are just by nature the most skeptical and careful people in our world, they don't say something unless it's been confirmed and double-confirmed, and these are people who are discovering things at such a rapid pace, they feel that they're closing in on the disease. I wasn't around to investigate Alzheimer's fifteen or twenty years ago, but I know from talking to a lot of people that years ago there was no sense of hope they were going to cure it. And now there are millions and billions of dollars involved, drugs in the pipeline that they're testing, different strategies to try to do something about these plaques and tangles, all these very inventive approaches, and I think we're fairly close to the first wave of drugs that will severely hamper this disease. And that's a great story in itself.

People feel the need to fill the void of ignorance concerning the causes of Alzheimer's, and some of the suggestions for the causes of the disease include fluoride, amalgam tooth fillings, refined flour, polished rice, and apparently the most popular suggestion of all, aluminum.

Part of this is purely benign—people want to have an understanding of the cause, and when an idea floats in and resonates with people, they grab on to it. Aluminum was that kind of idea. Fifteen or twenty years ago, they discovered aluminum in the brains of Alzheimer's patients. Then a scientist mentioned it to someone at a cocktail party, and some nonscientist made the association that aluminum was causing Alzheimer's disease. Even though it wasn't true, it caught on. The actual explanation is that the brain is compromised by the disease and is letting in all of these things from the general bloodstream that shouldn't be getting into the brain. So aluminum does not cause Alzheimer's disease.

But the thrust of your question has to do with pseudoscience. People are afraid, and they are vulnerable to the suggestions of others who know how to prey on those fears. We live in a world that is grounded in scientific study, and there are people who take advantage of that world by subverting it and poking holes in the weaknesses of science and often by pretending to be scientists. You can tell pseudoscientists miles away because they have this bravado, they claim to know the truth, and they're certain about it. They'll tell you things that no one else can tell you, and they usually claim to be bucking the system, claiming that the system doesn't want you to know something for whatever reason. And just by the way they're behaving, without any caution or skepticism, you can tell that it's crap.

There are people who say that Alzheimer's doesn't really exist, or that it's caused by one or another modern substance, or by depression or stress, and that it can be cured by something simple — deep massage of the feet or a certain kind of tea or not eating or drinking some kind of herb or substance. It's infuriating to see people do this. I tend to hear not from the pseudoscientists themselves but from their victims — people who say, "I've got Alzheimer's, but it's okay since I know that if I take this certain kind of herb I can control it." It's hard to talk to these people, because they think they know something that's making them feel better and more empowered. Yet as someone who has looked into this, I have an obligation to be candid with these people and tell them, "I'm sorry for saying this, but that supposed cure doesn't work. I've looked at that particular claim, and it doesn't make sense." It's a function of this modern, complex world, where there are always going to be problems and multiple sources of information and contradictions, and some people will always be prey to these pseudoscientists who know how to push people's buttons.

Dutch researchers have found that people who took anti-inflammatory drugs like ibuprofen or naproxen for at least two years were only one-sixth as likely to get Alzheimer's as people who didn't take the drugs.

Now you're back to real science. That's real. To me that seemed like a very significant study. One thing we haven't said in our conversation is that if you open the door into the world of Alzheimer's science, it's not as if there are four or five studies that show this or that, there are four or five *thousand* studies that will show this or that. Any gymnasium could be filled to the rafters with the paperwork that has gone into this disease, and a lot of it is contradictory and hard to make sense of, but what's clear is that they haven't yet found something that will cure Alzheimer's or stop it in its tracks. But there *are* certain things that might slow down the disease a bit or stave it off. And it seems that anti-inflammatory drugs may either slow down the disease or keep certain people from getting it. It's not clear which people they will help or what the side effects are. So we can't issue a blanket recommendation: "Take two Advil a day and you won't get Alzheimer's disease." But there's a lot of work going on in this field, and I think we're going to be hearing about some breakthrough drugs soon. What they're probably going to do is find a way to intervene in the disease and stop the plaques from forming well before they understand all the questions about what causes them in the first place. So it will be simpler to cure Alzheimer's than to completely understand it.

In your book you present the fascinating notion that the short-circuiting of memory forces every Alzheimer's sufferer to be always in the Now, which you say leads to an actual heightening of consciousness. And this reminds me of the Zen Buddhist idea of the importance of existing in the moment, discovering that the infinite is in the finite of each instant. And regarding this, I found a wonderful quotation by the Zen scholar D. T. Suzuki, who writes: "Man is

a thinking reed but his great works are done when he is not calcu-
lating and thinking. 'Childlikeness' has to be restored with long
years of training in the art of self-forgetfulness. When this is at-
tained, man thinks yet he does not think. He thinks like the show-
ers coming down from the sky; he thinks like the waves rolling on
the ocean; he thinks like the stars illuminating the nightly heavens.
Indeed he is the showers, the ocean, the stars."

That's amazing. What I immediately thought of when you were
reading that was that the other group of people who intuitively
understand this are songwriters and improvisational musicians —
the whole intent is that you have to forget this whole body of
knowledge and go with the moment. And the more you try to
copy or remember or relate this to anything in the past, the less
you are in the moment and the more difficult it is to let things develop.

This was not an idea that occurred to me. It's something that
was brought to my attention by a person named Morris Friedell,
who has Alzheimer's disease. (He has written: "We who have
Alzheimer's can appreciate clouds, leaves, flowers as we never did
before.") I never thought I'd be creating controversy, but some
people did get upset when they read the section of the book
where I talk about this sense of being in the Now. To embrace this
concept, you have to be comfortable with the idea of contradic-
tion, that there can be more than one idea going on at the same
time: you have this horrible disease that nobody would wish on
themselves or their friends or even their enemies. And at the same
time people who find themselves suffering with Alzheimer's
sometimes experience the freshness of life that can last for a while
and, before they deteriorate to the next phase of the disease, can
really be quite profound. The way it was expressed to me is that
people would see the color of a beautiful flower and they'd look
away and they'd see the flower again but it wouldn't be "again" —
it would be the experiencing of the initial beauty of that color and
that natural form for the first time. And there is something profound about that type of experience as opposed to experiencing
something for the thirtieth or fortieth or one hundredth time and

have it become quite numbing and deadening. Habit smothers life. But when you experience this for the first time, it can be quite overwhelming and awesome.

Your book seems to have been a personal journey for you, and you write: "I migrated over several years' time from morbid fascination and dread of Alzheimer's to a new kind of peace and reconciliation." How did that happen to you?

I think that part of it is just getting past the fear that you have, which comes from ignorance of the disease. If you don't know about something, as we were saying before, you just fill in the blanks in your knowledge with this generic dread. Once you get to know the details of the disease and the patients and caregivers, it's not that the disease becomes less awful, but you realize that this is also a human experience, not just this organic brain disease. These plaques and tangles are erasing your brain, and scientists are tackling this monumental problem. But there are also people who are going through this very poignant and sad experience who are wringing a lot of life out of it, and who in many cases are getting closer to their parents for a while. There's a lot of intimacy that goes on with Alzheimer's, a lot of human connection that's ultimately caused by this sad loss. There's a humanity that envelops and surrounds the world of Alzheimer's that you feel once you're inside it. It is very moving. I wouldn't say it erases the dread of the disease, but it does make it more of a human experience. When you get this close to the core of humanity, you are humbled by it. It's a very special place to be.

PART TWO

REMEMBERING

Remember me.

William Shakespeare,
Hamlet (the ghost)

In his "Ode: Intimations of Immortality," William Words-worth writes:

> Our birth is but a sleep and a forgetting:
> The Soul that rises with us, our life's Star,
>   Hath had elsewhere its setting,
>   And cometh from afar:
>   Not in entire forgetfulness,
>   And not in utter nakedness,
> But trailing clouds of glory do we come
>   From God, who is our home.

These lines hearken back to Plato, who thought of memory as divine, and to his notion that the soul has a previous existence, one that we forget when we are born. It is interesting that Plato speaks of the Greek word for "truth"—*aletheia*—in its etymological sense of "no forgetting." And because we are all forgetting people, we must spend our lives endeavoring to reawaken and to recollect the truths, knowledge, and primordial reality we once possessed, as well as the lives we once, perhaps, lived. As the fifth century B.C.

Greek philosopher Empedocles, a believer in reincarnation, wrote of himself: "A wanderer exiled from the divine dwelling, I was already in former times a boy and a girl, a bush and a bird, a mute fish in the sea. . . . I am delivered forever from death."

At death we cross the river Lethe, whose name means "forgetfulness," into a realm of ignorance, unknowing, and sleep. Those who attain enlightenment and who drink from the lake of Mnemosyne—the goddess of Memory, the omniscient Mother of invention for all human arts—and who are inspired by the Muses—the children of Mnemosyne—can remember not only themselves but also the places and persons they have felt closest to, for liking, too, is remembering. In a Platonic sense, everything we can see, know, create, and do has already been seen, known, created, and done at the beginning of Time. "Knowledge easily acquired," Plato wrote, "is that which the enduring self had in an earlier life, so that it flows back easily." As the architect Louis Kahn once stated, "What was has always been. What is has always been. What will be has always been." And as John Lennon once sang, "Nothing you can know that isn't known / Nothing you can see that isn't shown." All you need is love . . . and a good memory.

In the sixth century B.C., the Greek poet Simonides of Ceos was attending a banquet at which he chanted a lyric poem in praise of the twin gods Castor and Pollux. After the recitation, he received word that two persons were asking for him outside. Retiring from the hall, he found no one; just at the moment he was preparing to return, the roof of the banquet hall collapsed, crushing all the guests inside to death. The bodies were too mangled to be identified by the relatives of the deceased. But Simonides had remembered where each of the guests was seated, so he was able to identify them all. This experience led the poet to develop the principles of the art of memory of which he is said to be the inventor.

In *The Art of Memory*, Frances Yates explains the classical art of memory as it evolved in ancient Greece and Rome. The general rule of this mnemonic technique as applied, for example, to the declamation of lengthy speeches consists in the orator's ability to create a spacious, well-lit memory-building with forecourt, living room, bedroom, parlor, hallway, and balconies and, while making a speech, to wander in imagination through the memory-building, attaching words and longer sections of the speech to the places memorized. In the words of Cicero, "The order of the places will preserve the order of the things, and the images of the things will denote the things themselves, and we shall employ the places and images respectively as a wax writing tablet and the letters written on it." Thus, instead of writing, reading, or learning by rote, one collects and recollects. (Plato famously criticized the invention of writing because he felt it would produce forgetfulness in the minds of those who used it.)

Aristotle taught the surprisingly modern idea that every memory consists of two aspects: a "likeness" or "image" that is visual in nature, and an emotional resonance or coloring that, as Mary Carruthers has explained in *The Medieval Craft of Memory*, serves to "hook" a particular memory into one or more of a person's existing networks of experience. (Strong emotions make strong memories.) Aristotle also believed that the seat of the mind was located not in the brain but in the heart. (It is curious that we speak of someone learning or repeating something by heart.) Whether by the heart or by the brain, there are, of course, throughout history innumerable examples of prodigious feats of memory. Homer, like the Icelandic and Finnish bards, recited his poems by heart. Cicero was apparently able to speak in the Roman Senate for many days without relying on notes. At the age of fourteen, Mozart attended two performances of Gregorio Allegri's *Miserere* and proceeded to sit and write out the complete score from memory. The orchestral conductor Arturo Toscanini was able to memorize every note for every instrument in more than one hundred operas and two hundred symphonies. Gabriel García Márquez was so enamored of the Mexican writer Juan Rulfo's novel *Pedro Páramo* that he learned this 120-page work by heart. As a college student at Cornell, the literary critic Harold Bloom, on one inebriated evening, was supposed to have recited Hart Crane's seventy-six-page poem *The Bridge* backward ("bone infant by bone—lifeward back us Lug / faith and—lust our of" et cetera). Professor Kathy Eden of Columbia University memorized *Ham-*

let when she was fifteen years old. The Russian poet Anna Akhmatova, afraid of arrest, wrote her great long poem *Requiem* (1935–1940), dedicated to her son Lev, who was imprisoned in the Gulag, on small scraps of paper—later burned. Akhmatova and ten of her friends then kept these portions in their memories for more than twenty years; she was finally able to write the poem down in 1954, after the death of Stalin.

In the Islamic tradition, a person who has memorized the entire 114 chapters of the Koran is given the honorific title *Hafiz* (meaning "guardian"). In an ancient Indian tantric exercise, a student is taught to make two speeches at the same time, one sentence spoken on one subject, the next sentence spoken on another subject, and the trainee is regarded as having succeeded when he can make six or seven simultaneous speeches. It has been demonstrated that as many as 50 percent of primary school–age children may possess eidetic memory—the ability to retain an accurate, detailed visual image of a complex scene or pattern—such that, shown a piece of paper with writing on it for several minutes, they can spell many of the words both forward and backward. (This gift is rare after puberty; Harold Bloom seems to have retained it.) And then there is the phenomenal memory ability seen in autistic children, who unable to do relatively simple addition and subtraction, can, for example, give the day of the week for any day of the twentieth century or even calculate days occurring over many centuries. It is said that calendar calculation abilities can range from five to forty thousand years! Regarding these savants' prodigious feats of memory, James L. McGaugh, in *Memory and Emotion*, writes:

> Understanding their brains could well provide critical insights into how all of us learn and remember. One obvious possibility is that the lack of development of some brain areas or processes may enable the excessive elaboration of other brain regions required for the expression of such unusual talents. Another more intriguing possibility is that all of us may have brains that could potentially allow such exceptional talents, but the normal functioning of our intact brains may prevent the expression of un-

usual talent. The many systems of our brains constantly interact in enabling us to acquire, retain, and use many kinds of information. Such interaction may inhibit the unique functioning of specific brain systems that would otherwise enable greater memory and creativity. Thus, perhaps all of our brains may have the capacity for monumental memories that enable special talents.

Perhaps the most remarkable example of the unfathomable power of memory is described by the Russian neurologist A. R. Luria. In an astonishing and now-famous case study entitled *The Mind of a Mnemonist*, Luria writes of a man named Shereshevskii, whom he designates S., a Russian journalist who was referred to him by S.'s newspaper editor. Every day the editor would hand out assignments, lengthy lists of information and places he wanted covered. Surprised that S. never took notes, and thinking of reproaching him for inattention, the editor was amazed when S. repeated each assignment word for word. S. expressed surprise when asked about his powers of recall because he assumed that his memory was no different from anyone else's. Nevertheless, the editor recommended him to a psychology laboratory to have studies done on his memory. That is where Luria first encountered him. In their first meeting, Luria recited a series of sixty and then seventy words and nonsense syllables. S. closed his eyes, stared off into space, and then repeated the items forward and backward. In future sessions that took place days and weeks apart—some of them even separated by fifteen and then twenty years—S. could recall those same words. According to Luria, S. either continued to see the words or converted them into visual images.

Take the following table:

6 6 8 0
5 4 3 2
1 6 8 4
7 9 3 5
4 2 3 7
3 8 9 1

```
1 0 0 2
3 4 5 1
2 7 6 8
1 9 2 6
2 9 6 7
5 5 2 0
x 0 1 x
```

After three minutes S. was able to reproduce these items verti-cally, horizontally, and diagonally (i.e., the groups of four num-bers running zigzag throughout the chart) both forward and backward. Also remarkable was S.'s irrepressible power of synes-thesia, which compelled him to see and even taste words, num-bers, and sounds. According to Luria, "Presented with a tone pitched at 250 cycles per second and having an amplitude of 64 decibels, S. saw a velvet cord with fibers jutting out on all sides. The cord was tinged with a delicate, pleasant, pink-orange hue." And each word and number elicited a graphic image. In S.'s own words: "When I hear the word *green*, a green flowerpot ap-pears; with the word *red* I see a man in a red shirt coming toward me. . . . Even numbers remind me of images. Take the number 1. This is a proud, well-built man; 2 is a high-spirited woman; 3 a gloomy person (why, I don't know), 6 a man with a swollen foot; 7 a man with a mustache; 8 a very stout woman—a sack within a sack. As for the number 87, what I see is a fat woman and a man twirling his mustache."

The secret of S.'s powers lay in his mastery of the mem-ory technique invented by Simonides twenty-five centuries previously—distributing the images he conjured up along an av-enue or street, at a house or a store window, and then simply start-ing on his mental peregrination: "I had just started from Mayakovsky Square when they gave me the word *Kremlin*, so I had to get myself off to the Kremlin. Okay, I can throw a rope across to it. . . . But right after that they gave me the word *poetry* and once again I found myself on Pushkin Square. If I'd been given *American Indian*, I'd have had to get to America. I could, of course, throw a rope across the ocean, but it's so exhausting traveling."

Most uncanny of all was the manner in which he recalled a meaningless mathematical formula:

$$N \cdot \sqrt{d^2 \times \frac{85}{vx}} \cdot \sqrt[3]{\frac{276^2 \cdot 86x}{n^2v \cdot \pi 264}} \ n^2b = sv \ \frac{1624}{32^2} \cdot r^2s$$

S. studied the formula, shut his eyes, looked the material over in his mind, and minutes later reproduced it. The following account explains his astonishing method of recall:

Neiman (N) came out and jabbed at the ground with his cane ($\bullet$). He looked up at a tall tree, which resembled the square root sign ($\sqrt{}$), and thought to himself: "No wonder the tree has withered and begun to expose its roots. After all, it is here that I built these two houses" (d^2). Once again he poked with his cane ($\bullet$). Then he said: "The houses are old, I'll have to get rid of them ($\times$); the sale will bring far more money." He had originally invested 85,000 in them (85). Then I see the roof of the house detached ($-$), while down below on the street I see a man playing the Termenvox (vx). He's standing near a mailbox, and on the corner there's a large stone ($\bullet$), which had been put there to keep carts from crushing up against the houses. Here, then, is the square, over there the large tree ($\sqrt{}$) with three jackdaws ($\sqrt[3]{}$) on it. I simply put the figures 276 here, and a square box containing cigarettes in the square (^{2}). The number 86 is written on the box. (This number was also written on the other side of the box, but since I couldn't see it from where I stood I omitted it when I recalled the formula.) As for the x, this is a stranger in a black mantle. He is walking toward a fence beyond which is a women's gymnasia. He wants to find some way of getting over the fence ($-\!-\!-$); he has a rendezvous with one of the women students (n), an elegant young thing who's wearing a gray dress. He's talking as he tries to kick down the boards in the fence with one foot, while with the other (^{2})—oh, but the girl he runs into turns out to be a different one. She's ugly—phooey! (v). . . . At this point I'm carried back to Rezhitsa, to my classroom with the big blackboard. . . . I see a cord swinging back and forth there and I put a stop to that ($\bullet$). On the board I see the figure $\pi264$, and I write after it n^2b.

Here I'm back in school. My wife has given me a ruler (=). I myself, Solomon-Veniaminovich (sv), am sitting there in the class. I see that a friend of mine has written down the figure $1624/32^2$. I'm trying to see what else he's written, but behind me are two students, girls (r^2), who are also copying and making noise so that he won't notice them. "Sh," I say. "Quiet!" (s).

In this way, S. managed to reproduce the formula error-free. Fifteen years later, when Luria requested that he recall that same mathematical formula, S. did so in precise detail, spontaneously and without preparation!

S.'s overwrought memory is echoed and exemplified in Jorge Luis Borges's marvelous story "Funes, the Memorious," a tale of a man who for his first nineteen years lives in a memoryless, dreamlike state, hardly seeing or hearing anything and forgetting whatever is said to him. One day, thrown by a horse, he returns to consciousness remembering *everything*—every leaf on every tree and even every time he has perceived each leaf, also remembering each moment of his remembering: "We in a glance, perceive three wine glasses on the table; Funes saw all the shoots, clusters, and grapes of the vine. He remembered the shapes of the clouds in the south at dawn on the 30th of April of 1882. . . . He could reconstruct all his dreams, all his fancies. Two or three times he had reconstructed an entire day. He told me: *I have more memories in myself alone than all men have had since the world was a world.* . . . And again: *My dreams are like your vigils.* And again, toward dawn: *My memory, sir, is like a garbage disposal.*"

Like Funes, S., who sees and remembers everything, lives in a state in which sentences are cluttered with irrelevancies, filled with endless digressions, and riddled with inconsequential details . . . details producing even more details. Like Funes, he sees the leaves but not the trees, the trees but not the forest. He is unable to make discriminations, makes sense of almost nothing, and automatically turns every idea into an image or a color. He also cannot engage in meaningful human relationships because of his inability to separate his recollections of people into those of specific individuals. Unable to hold a job, he eventually becomes a professional mnemonist. As Luria concluded: "One would be hard put to say which was more real for him: the world of imagination in which he lived, or the world of reality in which he was but a temporary guest."

In order to control his pullulating sensations and thoughts, S. attempts fruitlessly to discover a technique of forgetting. While most people write things down in order to remember, S. makes note of the things he has no need to remember—phone numbers, last names. But in his mind he continues to see what he has written, and he eventually tries burning pieces of paper on which are noted the names and numbers he wishes to forget, only to discover their traces on the charred embers!

Fortunately, most people desire to master not the art of forgetting but rather the art of remembering. Marcel Proust did just this when one day, after tasting a now-legendary lime-perfumed *petite madeleine* dipped in tea, he experienced the ecstasy of a childhood recaptured, for with time momentarily suspended, he was instantly reawakened to those idle Sunday mornings in the French village of Combray when his aunt Léonie gave him madeleines and tea. Proust sensed that the past *is* the present because, as a scientist once said, "Each moment exists for always somewhere in space-time." As Proust writes: "When from a long-distant past nothing subsists, after the people are dead, after the things are broken and scattered, still, alone, more fragile but with more vitality, more insubstantial, more persistent, more faithful, the smell and taste of things remain poised a long time, like souls, ready to remind us, waiting and hoping for their moment, amid the ruins of all the rest; and bear unfaltering, in the tiny and almost impalpable drop of their essence, the endless edifice of recollection."

There is another wonderful story about time regained by another French writer, Jean Cocteau, who in his *Diary of an Unknown* describes walking down the street in Paris where he had lived as a child. Finding his old house, he makes his way to the backyard, where he notices how tall the trees have grown. A suspicious concierge calls out from a window asking him what he's doing there. Cocteau replies he's looking for his past and is summarily asked to depart. Not wanting to give up his quest, he remembers the times when, as a little boy, he would walk along the street close to the houses, trailing his hand against the walls and serrated gates, his fingers jumping from one spike to another. Trying to do this now, he feels nothing. But reminding himself that he had been smaller as a child, he bends down, closes his eyes, and runs his hand along the wall two feet off the ground. Suddenly and miraculously his former world comes back to him: "Just as the needle picks up the melody from the record," Cocteau writes, "I obtained the melody of the past with my hand. I found everything: my cape, the leather of my satchel, the names of my friends and of my teachers, certain expressions I had used, the sound of my grandfather's voice, the smell of his beard, the smell of my sister's dresses and of my mother's gown."

Someone once commented, perhaps only half-jokingly, that Cocteau's memory was actually in the wall. "Let us make Cocteau repeat his experiment," wrote the psychologist J. H. van den Berg, "but pay more critical attention this time to what the wall—the wall of the bricklayer—has to say." It is an enticing notion and one to meditate on. (I think that walls harbor many memories.) As Jorge Luis Borges once pointed out, however, the taste of an apple is not in the apple or in the eater but rather in the contact between them. And of course it was Proust's tongue and Cocteau's fingers and their contact with madeleine and wall that brought them back to their childhoods. Simply, their stories remind us that memory is the place where the present touches the past.

CHAPTER FOUR

ON MEMORY ENHANCEMENT
A CONVERSATION WITH CYNTHIA R. GREEN

Whatever it is you are struggling to remember
it is not poised on the tip of your tongue.

Billy Collins,
"Forgetfulness"

FOR PLATO, THE ENLIGHTENED NEVER LOSE THE VISION OF TRUTH and therefore have no need to remember. But for Cynthia R. Green, "forgetting is part of being human." Green is on the faculty of the Mount Sinai Medical School and the Mount Sinai Medical Center in New York City and is the founder of the Memory Enhancement Program at Mount Sinai Hospital—a memory wellness program for healthy adults consisting of six weekly classes that follows the principles of her book, *Total Memory Workout: Eight Easy Steps to Maximum Memory Fitness*, which draws on the latest neuroscientific research about its subject.

In clearheaded fashion, Green writes of lifestyle factors most likely to lower one's memory potential, such as lack of physical activity, poor diet, fatigue, depression, anxiety, and stress; suggests memory tools, such as schedulers, master plans, to-do lists, nag notes, forget-me-not spots, perpetual calendars, and locator logs; and explains internal memory techniques, such as rhyming, first letter association, repetition, storytelling, visual associations, and linking, which requires a person to organize five to nine "chunks" of numbers into smaller units—all of these underpinned by and applying Green's "A.M. principle," what she calls her program's "golden rule," designating *attention* and *meaning*, the finding and imposing of meaning on the information one wants to remember.

I found Green's approach both useful and effective, and she spoke to me about it in her office at the Mount Sinai Medical Center.

Supposedly the oldest memory book in the world, Ad Herennium, *was written in the first century* B.C., *so forgetfulness and the desire for memory improvement go back a long way. But why do you think that over the past twenty-five years there has been such a proliferation of memory books and memory improvement programs?*

There are probably two reasons. One is that we're faced with an aging population—the baby boomers are hitting their fifties and are now the largest segment of the American population; and in the same way that we saw a fitness boom when the baby boomers were in their thirties, we're seeing a memory fitness boom now that people in their fifties are starting to deal with issues concerning aging and the change of the memory function.

The other reason is that we live in an age in which we get information very quickly, tend to compare ourselves to computers, and expect to function at a very rapid rate, which taxes what we as humans are able to do. We can't learn and recall information like a computer. But I think we have that comparison, and the technology exposes us to a great deal more information than what people were exposed to in a previous generation. And this has spawned interest in memory and memory wellness.

I've been reading about the plasticity of the brain such that if synaptic connections are damaged, there can sometimes be compensatory synapse growth. So isn't it possible that a memory program like yours can help to generate new synapses?

To me, as a memory fitness expert and a gerontologist, that makes a lot of sense, because after all, there has to be some kind of physiological change representative of learning. When you learn something, something must change in the brain; and people can continue to learn until the day they die. In fact, Cameron Camp, among others, has demonstrated that even people at later stages of Alzheimer's disease are capable of learning. They may not be learning or operating at a more sophisticated level or at a level that they can function independently, but even with significant deterioration there can still be some learning possibilities.

Might it be fair to say that if you increase your memory you can increase your basic intelligence and cognitive abilities?

I think that's a tricky thing. What is intelligence? That's not an easy-to-answer question. According to the work of Howard Gardner on multiple intelligences, maybe what we measure traditionally as intelligence, using something like the Wechsler Adult Intelligence Scale, doesn't really capture all aspects of intelligence, and perhaps we haven't appreciated intelligence in other forms that we don't necessarily measure when we look at things that are more academic and that have to do with learning. So we have to question what is intelligence and the relationship of intelligence to memory.

What about the improvement of a person's cognitive ability?

There may be a correlation between a person's cognitive abilities and his or her memory function. For example, attention, which I consider to be very basic to good memory, is one of the most sensitive aspects of all cognitive functions; and if you have poor attentional ability, it's going to affect different aspects of your cognitive function. Conversely, if you have good attentional skills, that will probably benefit your overall cognitive functions, not just your memory function. However, I don't think you can therefore make the argument that good memory results in better cognitive function across the board. I think it's more complex than that.

The science writer George Johnson has described an experiment in which mice were bred with a lack of certain chemical receptors (NMDA) that link neurons in a region of the hippocampus, and the mice showed significantly diminished memory abilities. But when they were exposed to a stimulating environment, filled with toys and exercise wheels, they got their memory back. So it seems that exercising the brain's memory functions can overcome memory disuse; and that seems to agree with what you suggest in your book.

Of course it's a matter of use it or lose it. I really think it's a matter of recognizing that in the same way we take care of ourselves physically in order to live healthier lives, we need to practice good memory habits.

In your list of factors that can lower your memory potential, you mention information fatigue syndrome (or information overload). It has been suggested that our shorter attention spans have been partially brought about by the immersion of our minds in TV and computer screens.

I wouldn't be able to comment about that without reading the original source, but I think certainly if you look at our children developmentally and what they're exposed to, it's clear that what they focus on requires them to do so for far less time in order to get information. They're playing games or watching TV, and they don't need to stay focused on that information for as long as they require for reading.

In your book you advise people to take a good daily multivitamin and an antioxidant like vitamin E, but you seem skeptical of supplements like ginkgo biloba, choline, L-carnitine, and vinpocetine, which some people claim have positive effects on memory improvement.

One of the reasons I wrote my book and started the Memory Enhancement Program at Mount Sinai Hospital was because so much that was out there for the lay public was not scientifically based. The nutritional supplement business is a multibillion-dollar industry that is unregulated and is not overseen by any government agency. There's a real need for a program on memory wellness to be out there that is based on scientific research. And if you look at how to have a healthy memory function for average healthy adults—not those who have had memory problems because of serious illness or trauma—it's simply a matter of fitness. And in the same way you can't pop a pill to give yourself a great physique with great cardiovascular function, you can't expect to pop a pill for perfect memory function. It's just not realistic.

What about recent medications, like Aricept and Exelon?

Those are for people who have a diagnosed memory disorder like Alzheimer's disease and are currently being evaluated in people who have what we call "mild cognitive impairment," but these still are people who have demonstrated upon evaluation significant loss of memory function, and that may put them at greater risk for something like Alzheimer's. These pills are not for the run-of-the-mill person who is forgetting small things or has some mild changes in short-term memory with aging.

In your book you write about diets related to memory, about memory tools, and about memory techniques. But you don't seem to recommend as a memory tool something like the phonetic tag system, which as I understand it, assigns consonant sounds to numbers (0 through 9), then switches numbers with letters (t = 1, m = 2, n = 3), and then turns the letters into words.

For people who do it, it works great. But it's for people who either have a lot of time on their hands or do it professionally. Some people I know will use numbers 0 through 10 or 1 through 25, and they'll have those pegs that they work with. But I think for the average person it's too complicated.

Do you feel the same way about the so-called loci (place) system developed by Simonides and Cicero, among others, that assigns objects or words to places in a house or room, which one then walks through in one's mind?

Like any kind of system, it can work great if you use it. What I felt was more important was to provide the average person with short, simple techniques that he or she could really master quickly and use. The peg and loci systems are very effective, but I think it's discouraging for people who try to learn those techniques.

You say that the "golden rule" of your book is the A.M. principle, i.e., paying attention and giving meaning to what you're trying to remember. How did you come to formulate such a simple and basic formula?

In addition to my training as a psychologist, I've had the experience of working with a large number of people with memory disorders, as well as looking at the literature and seeing what works. And it became very clear that those were the two essential steps. It's not that I have a secret, it's pretty commonsense stuff, and it's just a matter of spelling it out for people so they can see it in that way.

You mention that the leading memory complaint of Americans is the inability to learn and remember names.

And it's obvious why. Because it's embarrassing when you forget a name, it's very public. I always say to my classes, If you forget what you put on your grocery list, nobody else knows. It's not as if you go to the checkout person and she tests you on whether you've gotten everything you needed at the store.

What are some of the practical techniques that you would suggest to help in remembering names?

The most basic one is the repetition technique, such that when you hear a name you repeat it back. So if I meet you at a function like a workshop, I would say, "Hello, Jonathan, nice to meet you," because by knowing that I'm going to need to repeat your name, I'll be focusing on it better, and by repeating your name I'm getting a chance to practice it.

Another very simple technique is to make a connection to the name, to something you already know, another person in your life or maybe someone famous. For example, my brother's name is Jonathan, so I can meet you again at that same event and can think to myself, Oh, Jonathan, like my brother's name, thereby making a connection between your name and the name of someone I know well. In that way I'm giving the name meaning that it would not have otherwise. So what I've done is describe the application of the A.M. principle to names—improving your attention and giving the information meaning.

Storytelling is another wonderful technique, in which you weave a small story or make up a ditty that provides a verbal association for the name, gives it meaning, and makes it more memorable. It takes a little bit more of a creative effort, but it allows you to give the name meaning, making it less likely to be forgotten: "Jonathan sells cots." That's not exactly your name, but it's going to get close enough to give it meaning. One of the examples I always use is Frank Hill, and one of my students came up with the following: "Frankly he's getting over the hill." It's a great way of giving meaning and making it memorable.

And one final technique is a visual analogue to that, what I call Making a Movie. In your mind's eye you make up a little visual story for the name. So for Frank Hill, someone might see frankfurters marching over a hill. There's motion to it, and it's like a little commercial for the name.

What do you do with people who you think have very serious memory problems? You say that, after the age of forty, people's memories tend to diminish. What is the fine line between normal memory loss and serious memory problems?

In my book I have a section in which I answer three frequently asked questions about this. The first question is: Does your forgetfulness get in the way of your performance at work or make it difficult for you to manage at home with your finances, hobbies, or other activities? And most of us who do assessments look at the question of whether something is just a normal change that may come with age or some other kind of functional problem, like depression or stress or normal life changes, as opposed to a true occurrence of early dementia. Look at the issue of functioning, and notice whether these changes are really getting in the way of the ability to function. That's a very important concept.

The second question you ask is: Has your memory gotten progressively worse over a period of time, such as six months? Is this a revealing sign?

It is, because we might all have some variability in our memory function. Maybe someone is having a lot of stress at work and is therefore more forgetful and more distracted. He forgets to put his kid's lunch in the lunch bag, she forgets an important meeting. So it may just be because of that stressor, and when that's relaxed or removed in some way, such that things get better at work or she changes jobs, what was perceived as a memory problem will then get better, too. It's situational. Whereas if it's a primary memory disorder that is developing, it will clearly progress and get worse over time.

Your third question is: Are your family and friends also worried about what these memory changes mean?

If you come in complaining of a memory problem at forty, there may be, as I said, other things causing the problem. But chances are that primary progressive dementia is not the first guess the clinician would make, because your risk of developing Alzheimer's disease at that age is very low. But if you're seventy-five, your risk is much greater. So most people who are in their seventies may have a family member whom they turn to for help and who is perhaps aware of their functioning. And often people who have an early stage of a memory disorder aren't aware of the changes that are occurring to them. They don't have that ability for self-awareness. So it's very important, in terms of making a diagnosis, to have input from a relative or a friend, someone who sees the person about ten hours a week, to give information about whether that person is forgetting more than usual.

Personally speaking, one of the reasons as a clinician I was drawn to doing this kind of work was to develop the ability to help more people and to allay fears, because for many people it is just a matter of understanding what memory is, how it works, and how we can keep our memories healthy.

CHAPTER FIVE

ON THE NEUROLOGY OF MEMORY
A CONVERSATION WITH RICHARD RESTAK

> Great is the power of memory, exceedingly great,
> O my God, a spreading limitless room within me.
> Who can reach its uttermost depth?
>
> Saint Augustine,
> *Confessions*

THE NEUROPHYSIOLOGIST CHARLES SCOTT SHERRINGTON ONCE called the brain "an enchanted loom." Virginia Woolf unknowingly extended this metaphor, writing of memory as a seamstress who "runs her needle in and out, up and down, hither and thither." How accurate she was. Memory is not a substance but a modular set of functions, a system whose distributed pieces are woven together on demand. Memories are not localized in a particular brain region but are diffused across many sites of the brain. Different parts of the brain are responsible for different memories, such that remembering your high school graduation depends on different brain networks than those for recalling where you left your misplaced eyeglasses. There are different memories for sounds, for sights, for smells. There is not one central memory command center, one imperial memory autocrat with slavish minions doing its bidding.

In order to explore the enchanted realm of memory, I spoke to Dr. Richard Restak, neuropsychiatrist and clinical professor of neurology at George Washington University Medical Center in Washington, D.C., and author of *The Modular Brain, The Brain Has a Mind of Its Own*, the bestselling *The Secret Life of the Brain* (a companion volume to the five-part PBS series of the same name), and *Mozart's Brain and the Fighter Pilot,* a lively, clearly written, and wide-ranging work drawing on music, literature, psychology, art, and philosophy that provides practical ways to increase concentration, powers of logic, problem-solving abilities, mental endurance, metacognition, sensory capacities, and of course, memory. "Try listening to Mozart for a few minutes each day," he writes. "You will find, in Bernard Shaw's words, 'music is really tapping into an inherent structure in the brain.' Perhaps Mozart can help you develop the ability to engage in multilevel thinking and thus use your brain in more creative ways."

Richard Restak spoke to me from his office in Washington, D.C.

It's been said that rather than one there are multiple *memory systems in the brain.*

That's right. Memory is a distributed function—that's a key and important thing. By that I mean it's not localized somewhere. So I may say to you, Let's talk a little bit about your college graduation, tell me what it was like. And you then tell me all sorts of things about it. If I had asked you the question five years ago, you probably would have been able to tell me a little bit more, and if I had asked you the day after the graduation, you'd have been able to fill in all kinds of details about who was there and so on. So your loss of memory is not like something going off a radar screen, it's what they call "graceful degradation," you just begin to get less clear and less specific: "What was the name of that guy who roomed next to me? I can't remember his name." Well, you would have known his name immediately if someone had asked you a couple of months after you graduated. So the memory is distributed. A lot of people have acted on the assumption that it's localizable, like Sherlock Holmes talking about the attic: if you want to move new things in, you have to move old things out. But it doesn't really work that way. It's just the opposite. The more you have, the more connections and linkages you can make. So it's the synapses and the neurons together that form the organ called the brain. The separate parts of information and experience *synapse* together, if you will, and they form mind and they form memory.

It's said that memories are imperfect reconstructions of our experiences. We remember how we have experienced not the events themselves but rather the remembering of something. One might even say that the act of remembering itself creates a brand-new memory of that memory.

That's correct. And that's why some people now are saying you can modify therapeutically certain experiences that were painful because each time someone brings them up and talks about them, he or she is reformulating them and then they're going to be encoded again, and if you interfere with that encoding, then you will interfere with the memory and a person won't remember them as well. There's a lot of research being done on that, and there's some controversy about whether or not this is true. But as you just phrased it, that's correct, you're reformulating the memory, and you can prove that. If you get someone to describe a scene and then, through your questioning, modify a critical point in that scene, then that's how he or she will remember it. Take the example of a car accident. Someone will drive through a stop sign and be in a collision. Later when you're interviewing the driver you say, Well, the other person didn't stop at the red light, right? And the person doesn't remember there wasn't a red light, it was a stop sign, and he'll say, That's right, the driver went right through the light. And that's how he'll remember it forever. He will be totally convinced that the intersection was controlled by a stoplight rather than by a stop sign.

In a way it's something like remembering a photograph of an event rather than the event itself.

I'm kind of uncomfortable with photographs and video as metaphors for memory. They're too static. You can't modify what's in a photograph; you can't really modify what's on a video either in any meaningful way in terms of context and things like that. It's a more dynamic process, it's modifiable by experience, and a lot of the confusion about it stems from the work of Wilder Penfield when he was electrically stimulating his patients and getting them to remember specific memories and events. But many of those things were composites, they weren't a specific afternoon-in-the-yard-playing-with-friends, it was more like many afternoons playing with friends and children.

Apparently the brain changes its connective patterns every second of our lives in response to everything we experience, so that when you speak to someone on the phone or go to see a movie, your brain has changed. This is a pretty amazing notion.

It is. However, that has to be supplemented with the fact that there usually have to be other things done to make sure that this insight is acted upon. You look back in history, and certain historic persons have experiences—Saul on the road to Damascus is catapulted from a horse, he gets up and hears God and becomes an apostle—that would be an example of an experience that had such an overwhelming effect on him that it did change his whole life. These things can occur. And your brain is changing moment to moment as you're reading and talking. Well, we've all had powerful conversations and learned things, but the concept is more along the lines that in each moment the brain and memory are being changed and altered a little bit, they're not the same as they were a few minutes ago. And they're everlastingly dynamic. But it's not necessarily a question of better and better and bigger and bigger, because as we know, as people get older we lose a lot of our memories.

Everyone who talks about memory refers to the hippocampus—one of the major structures of the so-called limbic system—as crucial to an understanding of memory. The hippocampus is the place where memories are initially encoded and consolidated, and in Alzhei-

mer's disease the hippocampus is the first thing to be damaged, and
even stress can damage it. Could you say something about the
hippocampus?

The hippocampus is the entry point for memory—this is where
you encode the information so that it becomes a message, if you
will, and then it's distributed. So you can think of the hippocampus as the distribution center. We talked earlier about the memory being distributed and spread throughout the brain, and it
comes into the hippocampus, where the encoding takes place.
And recently it's been found that prolonged stress and certain
types of depression will cause loss of cells. The hippocampus gets
smaller—you can see it on the MRI—and it's interesting that a lot
of patients come in complaining about their memory. Every neurologist and psychiatrist has had the experience of seeing someone whom he or she thought was becoming demented but also
recognized the patient's depression and said, Well, let's treat the
depression and we'll do what we can about the dementia later.
And then a couple of weeks later the person will come back and
the so-called dementia is gone because the inability to remember
was part of the depression. If you looked at the hippocampus,
you'd find that it has rejuvenated itself, there are more connections.

After being encoded in the hippocampus, where do the memories
ultimately go to be stored as long-term memories?

They get distributed. Think of the hologram. When you begin to
see a less sophisticated hologram, you don't have the whole
image disappear, it just becomes grainier, it becomes less precise.
That's what happens to memory. You're not going to find it in any
one place, you're not going to say, Where's the memory?
    When you're talking about some event, the visual component
of it is probably more strongly encoded within the visual area
than in the auditory area. And when you're talking about what
things sounded like or felt like, then you probably have referen-
tial coding in the auditory areas. But it's still distributed because

we don't experience life in terms of separate sights, sounds, feel-ings, it's all integrated into one experience, so it's got to be in the association cortex. And of course the association cortex is the largest area, it's much bigger than any localized area.

It's said that sleep associated with REM dreaming helps to form and consolidate memories, and without this kind of dreaming, long-term memories sometimes have trouble being formed and stored.

You can disrupt memory by frequently awakening people. It used to be believed that you can learn things in your sleep, that you could go to bed with a tape on, playing foreign languages. But this practice has never been shown to be effective. So memory is sorted, it's filtered. Also, REM deprivation leads to a lot of psychi-atric problems such that the patient begins to become either irri-table or violent. During those fund-raising efforts when people stay up for a week or so—they're all eventually carted off delu-sional and hallucinating. And of course they get better when they get some sleep.

Along with the hippocampus, the frontal lobe in particular seems to be important for memory.

The most important function of the frontal lobe has to do with working memory. And working memory is simply—to use a com-puter term—keeping something online while you're working on something else. After you read a long sentence by Proust, it's the working memory that keeps the first part of the sentence online so that you can link it to the rest of the sentence and get a whole meaning out of it. That's why certain writers are so hard to read, because they demand so much working memory; the sentence can be so long, so intricate, so self-referential that it makes read-ing it difficult. And that's working memory.

When you have frontal lobe lesions, you have a problem keeping more than one thing in mind at the same time. Let me give you an example: I have a patient who was in a bicycle accident, hit the back of her head, and now has some frontal lobe damage. And what she's done is give up her job as a manager and is now working as a clerk. And I said to her, "What do you find about the clerking job that makes it so much easier than the other job?" And she said to me, "I only have to deal with one thing at a time. I don't have to deal with different people coming up to me about different things, somebody on the telephone, somebody standing in front of me wanting to give me a message, my beeper going off." And that's working memory. It's linking things in time.

There's something called future memory. What is that?

I'll give you an example: Young people are not sure what they want to do with their lives, and they meet a neurosurgeon who says, Come into the hospital and I'll show you some things. And they're so impressed with everything that they decide they want to become neurosurgeons. They start medical school and residency, and then there are certain days when they think, This isn't worth it, why did I ever get into this? And the future memory is that part that revives, and they feel again what they experienced when they made up their minds about what they wanted to do. They don't just live in the moment, they know they're having a rough time, but they have their goal in mind and want to achieve it.

You've said that if we allow our emotional memories to disappear, we eventually lose touch with ourselves. What is emotional memory?

Emotional memory could also be called experiential memory. If I asked you about something that happened earlier today, not only would you be able to tell me but you'd be able to feel the same way you did about the situation a few hours ago—not only is it a picture in your mind but you're linked to it. If I ask you about yesterday, you might be able to remember as well. But if I get back much further, then you'll really be able to link up to only things that were emotionally intense for some reason or another. Just last week I went to a funeral, for my aunt, and there was the casket and they were playing some beautiful music, "Our Lady of Knock," it's an Irish song—my aunt was Irish—and it was very moving. And then I wondered why I was so emotionally involved in this, and I realized as I was sitting there listening to the service that I was going back over all the times I had known my aunt when I was a child, an adolescent, and a young adult. And I realized that this was probably the first time I had ever sat down and thought that much about my aunt. So that's where the emotional part came in. My emotional memory came flooding back, and it was very powerful. At a funeral people don't just think of people, they really begin to experience what it was like to have known and interacted with them over the years. How often do you sit down and really think about your experiences with somebody? And perhaps we should do this at times other than when people have died. And that's the emotional memory, sitting in the pew for a period of time, hearing this music, thinking about my aunt, and suddenly remembering her with a much greater intensity than I would have a week or two earlier.

What is the difference between declarative or explicit memory and nondeclarative or implicit memory?

Declarative means just that. Tell me who was the sixteenth president of the United States. And the person responds that it was Abraham Lincoln. You can declare it, you can say it, it's explicitly put forth, there it is. But if you ask, Who's the sixteenth president of the United States, and the person says, Gosh, I know who that is, give me a minute, he's on the five-dollar bill, wait, don't tell me—then you're sort of in between explicit and implicit memory, you know it but you can't quite get it out. And suddenly it comes to you. The more usual explanation of implicit memory is also a form of operational memory—shooting pool, riding a bicycle. They're things that are nondeclarative, you can't tell someone how to ride a bicycle. But you can set up a circuit which will remain inactive perhaps for years. But, for instance, I once wrote an essay about my getting on a bicycle after not having been on one for years, and suddenly I started to panic as I was going down a hill. But then the whole thing clicked right in, the program came on, and I was riding again.

What is the difference between episodic memory and semantic memory?

An episodic memory is: Tell me what you did yesterday, and you can know that something happened and you can describe it. A semantic memory is something you know that you perhaps have never explicated to yourself. For instance, to be president of the United States, you have to have been born in the United States. You probably know that, but you don't remember when you read it. The episodic memory is something you can often account for in terms of what happened, where and when, and that kind of thing, but semantic memory is where you can't tell me under what conditions and what time you learned that Lincoln was the sixteenth president. There's no way you can remember that. You learned it sometime when you took American history, but you can't say the day or time. And that's where the emotional part of it links in. Most of the time that we can remember the specific situation, that such and such a thing occurred, it's almost always something that has an emotional valence to it—a positive or negative limbic-based feeling. Because why else would you remember it? If you were learning the presidents of the United States in the fourth or fifth grade and suddenly someone outside the classroom was hit by a car and you ran to the window and looked out and saw someone run over, you may well be able to tell me when you learned who was the sixteenth president because that occasion was so memorable that that shift into episodic memory is no longer part of semantic memory.

And just to follow up on that: Take the term *psyched up*, as when someone says, "I've got to get psyched up." And what that really means is that if I'm getting ready for my exam and I'm sitting there pretty comfortably because I've been getting A's in all of my classes so far and think it's going to be an easy exam, I may wind up with a B, so for my next exam I've got to get *psyched up*, which is another way of saying that I have to get emotionally aroused so that I can do my best. Because if you're not alert and not really energized and have low-level anxiety, if you want to call it that, then you may be too laid-back and you may not do as well. And that's another example of taking something which is not inherently emotional and sort of emotionalizing it in order to embed it more clearly in your memory. The more you get that adrenaline flowing, the more you make the sympathetic nervous system get involved, the more likely you are to be able to encode something.

In your book Mozart's Brain and the Fighter Pilot, *you address the problem of the corresponding link between the increase of external memory devices, such as computers, calculators, and spell-checkers, and the diminishing of one's memory.*

It depends on what use you put them to. Let's say you carry around an audio recorder. It's a lot of fun just to turn it on, have a conversation, and later on do what Truman Capote used to do, which was to try to re-create the conversation exactly as it occurred word for word, and try to remember every bit of it. And then after you can't remember any more of it, turn on the recorder and listen to it. And that enhances your memory. Otherwise you're getting what we call "disuse atrophy." So the technology has a positive spin to it; it allows you to enhance your natural memory abilities. But it can be abused. I mean someone can say, Why bother to remember anything? Samuel Johnson said the key to mastery in memory is to know something or to know where to find it.

Now this also gets into the concept of whether there is in fact a fatigue factor. Have you ever had the experience where you're so tired and don't want to learn anything new? And you'll say, I'll just mark that page and come back to it later. And you know where it was. So if someone asks you about such and such and the book is there, you haven't read it yet but you can get to it, and there's the answer right there on the page. That's one kind of memory. The more respectable memory is to have assimilated the material and then be able to use it.

Plato thought that even writing could diminish one's memory powers.

In Homer's works you notice that each of the characters is consistently described with an adjective. Homer's epics, of course,
come from an oral tradition, and it was an early attempt to facili-
tate the encoding of names and situations by putting them into an
epithet. We, too, give epithets or nicknames to people; it's an easy
way to remember them. We talk about Slick Willy, Honest John,
Doubting Thomas. A nickname is a mnemonic device. And I
think it's one of the reasons that kids use nicknames so often for
each other. It's a way of distinguishing one child from another.

I have a patient who was in a serious auto accident—she
teaches preschool—and she was having a problem remembering
names and faces. And what she does at the start of every new year
is say to her pupils, Here's my picture when I was your age, and
tomorrow everyone bring in a recent picture of yourself. They
bring the pictures in, and she then uses the pictures to connect
with the names. And she practices this for hours and creates the
linkage. So she's developing a system, and I thought it was very
clever.

*It's said that short-term and long-term memories are different
processes mediated by different brain systems.*

There's some controversy about that. Suppose I ask you to repeat
to me seven digits forward and seven digits backward; we're testing your short-term memory. If I say to you later, "By the way, I
want to give you three words to remember—*apple*, *table*, and
penny," and I ask you to say them back to me and you say, "Apple,
table, penny. What's the big deal?" and I say, "Don't forget them
because I'm going to ask you to name them later." Then I go on
and say, "Spell the word *world* backward, tell me the presidents
from Bush back to Nixon," and then after that I say, "And by the
way, what were those three things I mentioned before?" Some
people can't come up with them, and they have a problem with
memory storage. Alzheimer's patients often can give you the
numbers back. I'll say to them "1, 2, 3, 4, 5" and ask them to say

the numbers backward—5, 4, 3, 2, 1—and they don't do too badly, but when I say, "Apple, table, penny, don't forget them," a minute later they don't have a clue what I'm talking about. When I ask them about those three things, they say, "What three things?" So their short-term memory and encoding process are severely affected.

Throughout Mozart's Brain and the Fighter Pilot *you make the point that if one learns a lot, the brain circuitry can change extensively, and that if you increase your memory, you increase your basic intelligence. What is the relationship between memory and cognition?*

We really are our memory, we are what we can remember, because that gives us the richness of life, our connection to the past. As you learn new pieces of information, you link them with other things, and either it's done automatically or it can be done deliberately because you're making a deliberate effort to link certain things together. And as a result you link past, present, and even future—we talked about future memory before. So that when you talk to people who have Alzheimer's disease, the most striking thing is the bleakness of their mental horizon because they live in the present and are unable to recall the past. They've lost a whole part of their being, they've lost a part of their soul, if you will. And then there is an enrichment that you can observe in someone who has developed a finely woven, intricate, complex network of associations that enables him or her to enter back into the past and remember things that occurred before and then link them to what is going on now and speculate about what is coming up next.

So it would be hard to imagine somebody who would be really intelligent in the full range of the meaning of that word yet suffered from a severe memory gap. Take a tournament chess player. How can anybody play chess who couldn't remember plays of his own or someone else's? I have the theory that you can actually enhance your intelligence by enhancing your memory. You *can* increase your IQ, but I'm thinking more about the ability to converse with people on a variety of topics that comes from learning and remembering and keeping things in mind and being able to bring them up in one's working memory.

Cognitive scientists often make the analogy between memory and the computer. But as William James once wrote, "Memory requires more than a mere dating of a fact in the past. It must be dated in my past. I must think that I directly experienced its occurrence. It must have warmth and intimacy." Computers obviously lack this sense of personal experiential reality, a reality that in computers is represented by processes such as storage and retrieval, input and output. What do you think of this analogy?

First of all, the computer is going to have a more powerful memory than any person, so in a contest the computer wins hands down. But it's a different kind of memory, it's a memory that doesn't have what you call a "metamemory." The metamemory is when you and I can switch our topic and start remembering different things—we can talk about a musical composition or we can switch and talk about boxing champions. The computer may have all that knowledge in there, but it's not going to be able to switch back and forth because it's not driven by a person, if you will. So it has all that information in there but doesn't know when to use it. William James is talking about the fact that the memory is linked up with the particular consciousness of a person, he's conscious not only of the event but of himself *remembering* the event. Obviously, the computer doesn't do that.

Here's a scene for you: A beautiful woman and a handsome man are sitting together playing a game of chess, and in the middle of the game the man looks over at the woman, turns the king down, signaling defeat, and winks at the woman. I mean, there's more conveyed there than just the surrendering of the king. There's no way a chess computer is ever going to understand the message the man is sending to the woman, which she's picking up on. So once again everything is contextualized. Only the human brain can contextualize and recontextualize things in such a way that they take on a totally different meaning.

CHAPTER SIX

ON FALSE AND RECOVERED MEMORIES

A CONVERSATION WITH RICHARD J. MCNALLY

> You, your mom, Tien and Tuan, all went to the
> Bremerton K-Mart. You must have been five years old
> at the time. Your mom gave each of you some money
> to get a blueberry ICEE. You ran ahead to get into
> the line first, and somehow you lost your way in
> the store. Tien found you crying to an elderly
> Chinese woman. You three then went together to
> get an ICEE.
>
> E. Loftus, J. Feldman, and R. Dashiell,
> "The Reality of Illusory Memories"

ONE OF THE FASCINATING THINGS THAT WE'VE DISCOVERED DUR-
ing the past forty years is that one can implant false memories in
people. The psychologist Elizabeth Loftus and her colleagues
have been able to convince about 25 percent of adult subjects
that when they were children they had found themselves lost
while shopping with relatives. With regard to the fabricated story
quoted above, the subject agreed that she had gotten lost and
elaborated: "I vaguely remember walking around . . . crying. I
thought I was lost forever. I went to the shoe department [and]
the handkerchief place. . . . I circled around the store it seemed
ten times. I just remember walking around and crying. I do not
remember the Chinese woman or the ICEE (but it would have
been raspberry ICEE . . .) part. I don't even remember being
found. . . . I just remember feeling that nobody was going to find
me. I was destined to be lost at Kmart forever."

Another example of an implanted false memory: a researcher created a fake photograph purportedly taken years earlier of a child and a grown-up sitting together in a hot-air balloon, and despite the fact that the trip had never occurred, half of the adult subjects shown such a picture of themselves recalled the balloon journey, munificently providing vivid details of the experience. My favorite act of memory persuasion, however, is the experiment conceived by Elizabeth Loftus and Jacquie Pickrell in which they convinced 30 percent of 120 adult subjects that they had encountered and shaken hands with Bugs Bunny—a Warner Bros. notable—in Disneyland.

Reflections on the nature of accuracy, suggestibility, and distortion in memory lead us to the highly contentious and often vitriolic debate between advocates of "recovered" memories—of, for example, childhood sexual abuse or of persons claiming they engaged in satanic cult rituals—and adamant opponents of these kinds of "memories," who assert that memory can often succumb to the power of suggestion by means of psychotherapists' use of hypnosis, trance induction, guided imagery, and age-regression techniques.

In 1992 the parents of a daughter who accused her father of sexual abuse founded the False Memory Syndrome Foundation to combat what they saw as the smearing of innocent persons by unscrupulous therapists. Those convinced about the unassailable truth of trauma amnesia, however, see such efforts as attempts by abusers to suppress the truth. In 1995 an American Psychological Association task force reviewed research on memory and repression and concluded that "absent other corroborating evidence, it is impossible to tell whether a memory is a real memory, partially real, or false, and that because of this point there is no way for science to determine the differences there." As the Harvard psychologist Daniel Schacter has remarked: "Searching for the truth in this charged atmosphere is not easy."

In his book *Remembering Trauma* (2003), Richard J. McNally, drawing on the latest scientific and clinical evidence (his book cites more than 1,200 works), has attempted the seemingly impossible task of searching for the truth about false and recovered memories. A clinical psychologist and professor of psychology at Harvard University, McNally has more than 230 publications to his credit, most concerning anxiety disorders, including the book *Panic Disorder: A Critical Analysis*.

Richard J. McNally spoke to me from his office at Harvard University's Department of Psychology.

It seems that it's relatively easy to implant false memories in people—adults being persuaded that as children they got lost in shopping malls, that they took rides in hot-air balloons, that they encountered Bugs Bunny in Disneyland. It seems that the act of imagining false events convinces people they actually happened, that the act of imagining makes an event familiar and this familiarity is later mistakenly remembered as a childhood experience.

Many psychologists will say that it is "easy" to implant false memories, but "easy" as compared to what? About 25 percent of subjects will develop false memories in these studies, but whether that strikes you as a lot or a little will depend on what your expectation is.

What do you think it is that makes some persons more susceptible to false memories than others?

Any psychological variable that makes it tough for a person to distinguish between memories and fantasies should increase a person's risk for developing false memories. For example, people who score high on the personality trait of *absorption* may be more likely than others to confuse imaginings with memories of real happenings. Absorption is related to fantasy proneness, hypnotizability (at least in some contexts), daydreaming, and imaginative engagement with everything from a good novel to an entrancing sunset. My research group has found that individuals who believe they have been abducted by space aliens score high on measures of absorption, and we strongly suspect that their abduction memories are false! The typical "abductee" experiences an episode of sleep paralysis accompanied by hypnopompic—"upon awakening"—

hallucinations of intruders in the bedroom. These harmless but often frightening events occur when a person awakens from rapid eye movement [REM] sleep, the stage of sleep when we do most of our dreaming. During REM, our body is paralyzed, but we don't know that because we are asleep. In any event, during one of these episodes the person awakens before the paralysis wanes and notices that he or she cannot move. Sometimes fragments of dreaming intrude into awareness—a kind of "dreaming with one's eyes open"—and the person hallucinates figures later interpreted as ghosts, angels, space aliens, and so forth. Many of our subjects then went to hypnotherapists, who "helped" them recover the missing memories of being whisked through bedroom windows up into spaceships, being medically probed, and whatnot. The point here is that these individuals score high on absorption, and this skill seems to increase the likelihood of their developing vivid imaginings that seem like real memories.

In Remembering Trauma *you suggest that true memories are usually accompanied by mere feelings of recollective experiences, whereas fake memories are usually accompanied by mere feelings of familiarity.*

That is not inevitably true, however. For example, our "alien abductee" subjects provided vivid memories of having been medically probed on spaceships—memories that are unlikely to be true. But the distinction between recollecting an experience and knowing that it must have occurred can be illustrated as follows. For example, let's say you always lock your door when you leave your house in the morning, and if someone says to you, "Did you lock your door this morning?" you reply, "Of course I did." "Well," the person asks, "do you actually recollect locking the door—can you relive the experience in your mind?—or do you just have a feeling that you must have locked it?"

There is a good chance that your confidence that you locked it is based on a vague sense that you must have done so rather than a vivid, recollective reliving of the memory. The more sensory details embedded in your recollection, the more likely it is that the memory reflects a genuine experience. But this rule of thumb is not infallible.

The confusion between memory and imagination can in reality have serious implications and consequences with regard to, among other things, clinical care, legal cases, and family relations, as when a parent is accused of sexual abuse. In Remembering Trauma *you mention the idea of "reality monitoring" with regard to the confusions that can accrue from the intermingling of memory and imagination. Could you say something about what reality monitoring means?*

"Reality monitoring" refers to the psychological processes that enable us to distinguish mental contents arising from perception from those arising from imagination—that is, to distinguish reality from fantasy. Reality monitoring skills help us answer questions like "Did this actually happen to me? Or did I just imagine it or dream it?" Individuals with poor reality monitoring skills may experience difficulty distinguishing memories of previous experiences from memories of experiences that were merely imagined. For example, some psychotherapists who suspect a client suffers from repressed memories of childhood sexual abuse will ask the client to visualize scenarios of possible abuse. A client with poor reality monitoring skills may subsequently confuse a memory of such visualized abuse with a memory based on a genuine event.

What do you think is the credibility of people's first memories? Are they mostly imaginary or real? Here's one of my favorites, from the director Ingmar Bergman's autobiography, The Magic Lantern: *"I am sitting on someone's knee being fed with gruel. The plate is on a grey oilcloth with a red border, the enamel white, with blue flowers on it, and reflecting the sparse light from the window. By bending my head sideways and forwards, I try out various viewpoints. As I move my head, the reflections in the gruel plate change and form new patterns. Suddenly, I vomit over everything. That is probably my very first memory."*

[Laughing] It's really hard to tell. Sometimes what will happen, for example, is that a child—say, at age nine—is sitting around the dinner table while his parents tell stories about his early childhood, including an unusual event occurring to him when he was two years old. While hearing this story retold, the child will likely generate visual imagery in response to the story. He may later come to mistake his memory of these images for a memory of the original event, which occurred much too early in his life for him to remember it now. He may then mistakenly claim that his earliest memory is from the age of two years, and that it is very vivid.

But I have a first memory from the age of four or five, which no one told me about, of sitting under the piano and listening to my mother play a Chopin prelude. You're not saying that all first memories are reconstructive, are you?

No, not at all. I'm not saying that they're always wrong, just that it's very difficult to distinguish as an adult between the "first memories" that do correspond to events you once experienced and encoded and those that you have heard about a few years later and then imagined and thought were the actual perceptual records of the original experiences. It's just that it's sometimes tough to tell them apart.

It's been said that powerful emotions can reinforce real memories, but false memories, once they're accepted, can themselves elicit strong emotions and mimic the real ones. There seems to be a complex relationship not only between memory and imagination but also between memory and emotion. Could you say something about that connection?

I mentioned our research with "alien abductees" earlier. Well, we wondered whether these individuals would exhibit all the physiological signs of intense emotional reliving—increased heart rate, sweating, facial muscle tension—when they recalled their most terrifying "abduction memories" in the laboratory. That is, would these folks exhibit the same heightened psychophysiological response that patients with post-traumatic stress disorder exhibit when they recall memories of combat events? Can a false traumatic memory produce the same type of emotional physiological reaction as a genuine traumatic memory? We used the same procedure that we use with Vietnam veterans and child abuse survivors: we had the "alien abductees" write down a narrative of their most traumatic encounters with aliens, and then some positive events, some other stressful events, and then some neutral ones, like mowing the lawn last Saturday. What we then did was to take all that material and convert it into thirty-second audiotape scripts. We played these scripts back to the "abductees" in the laboratory, asking them to imagine the experiences described. So, would someone who listens to an audiotaped description of his or her presumably false traumatic memory react like someone who hears an audiotaped description of a genuine traumatic memory? The answer is yes. In fact, the alien abductees showed very strong physiological reactions, at least as strong as those of real trauma patients. So here you have evidence that a false memory can drive a physiology hitherto attributable only to genuine traumatic events. The power of imagination is much stronger than many people suspect.

Do you think there may be a kind of parallel relationship between the implanting of false memories and the so-called recovery of false memories?

First of all, I don't think therapists "implant" false memories in any real sense of the word. I always cringe when I hear psychologists use that word *implant,* because it implies intention. Some therapists have unwittingly *fostered* false memories in some of their patients, but that's a different matter from *implanting* them.

There are certainly parallels between the methods researchers have used to implant (nontraumatic) memories in their subjects and the methods some therapists have used to uncover presumably repressed memories of abuse, thereby fostering the development of false memories. In both cases, a supposedly knowledgeable authority figure tells the person that a certain event—getting lost in a shopping mall, having been molested by one's grandfather—may have happened (or did happen). Guided imagery of the postulated events, for example, has been used in both the experimental and therapeutic contexts, sometimes with unintended adverse consequences in the latter, that is, when clients come to believe that their visualizations correspond to genuine traumatic events.

However, I do want to emphasize that a lot of people who report recovered memories of childhood sexual abuse do not recall these memories during psychotherapy. For example, in one of our recent projects, Dr. Susan Clancy and I studied twenty-seven adults who reported having been molested as children, not having thought about it for many years, and then having the experience come to mind, often after encountering a reminder. In most of these cases, the person had been fondled once or twice, and often had no idea what was going on. Only years later did the person realize that he or she had been molested. Few of these individuals said the experience was terrifying or traumatic at the time of its occurrence. They remember having been confused, upset, and disgusted but not terrified. But one-third of them today are deeply distressed by experiences they now recognize as abuse. Only now, fully understanding what had happened, they retrospectively reappraised the experience as traumatic. Incidentally, there is little reason to believe that these memories were "repressed" or "dissociated" from awareness or otherwise subject to amnesia. Indeed, not having thought about something for a long period of time is not the same thing as being unable to remember it, and inability to remember is the hallmark of amnesia. For instance, I could ask you about your second-grade gym teacher—

I didn't have a gym teacher in the second grade.

[Laughing] Bad question! Okay, but I could ask you about your second-grade teacher and say, "When was the last time you thought about that teacher?" You might say, "Wow, it must have been a decade ago!" But the mere fact that a memory of the teacher had not popped into your mind for ten years does not mean that it was "repressed" or otherwise inaccessible.

All of this is obviously what you mean when you write in the first pages of Remembering Trauma *that "people remember horrific experiences all too well. Victims are seldom incapable of remembering their trauma."*

Right.

And you continue: "People sometimes do not think about disturbing events for long periods of time, only to be reminded of them later. However, events that are experienced as overwhelmingly traumatic at the time of their occurrence rarely slip from awareness." But playing devil's advocate here for a moment, I notice you say "seldom incapable" and "rarely slip." What did you mean by those hedging words?

Never say *never* in the behavioral sciences! There is a small chance of an exception to the general rule turning up. I'm simply hedging my bets here because it's possible that there may very well be isolated cases of a person who has experienced something overwhelmingly terrifying at the time it occurred and was unable to remember it for many years. Every now and then one encounters hearsay, anecdotes of varying degrees of plausibility. But evidence for repression of genuinely traumatic memories ranges from the flimsy to the nonexistent.

You do say in your book that events that trigger overwhelming terror are memorable unless they occur in the first year or two of life or the victim suffers brain damage or has experienced extreme starvation or sleep deprivation during the experiencing of these events.

That would also be true. When I was using those hedge words *rarely* and *seldom*, I was implying that those other factors were not involved. But if someone, for example, experiences an earthquake in Turkey when he's two years old, he'll remember little or

nothing of this experience because of the developmental imma-
turity of his brain, not because he "repressed" the memory of the
quake.

*The French psychiatrist Pierre Janet wrote about a case in which a
woman would freeze in terror every time she passed a certain door
that led to the outside of her house and couldn't explain what
freaked her out about that spot. Later she found out that years before, some men had decided as a joke to tell her that her drunken
husband, whom they'd placed on the doorstep, was dead. Since
that time the woman associated that doorway with extreme fear. So
the traumatic event did slip from this woman's awareness.*

If one could actually verify that she was unable to remember it—
as opposed to being merely unwilling to talk about it—that would
be the type of rare case I was referring to.

*One of your conclusions in your book is that "there is no reason to
postulate a special mechanism of repression or dissociation to explain why people may not think about disturbing experiences for
long periods. A failure to think about something does not entail an
inability to remember it." That last statement seems incontrovert-
ible to me. Perhaps I'm just revealing my personal resistance, emotional or intellectual or both, but I do seem to have a resistance to
the notion that, as James L. McGaugh put it—and I gather that
you would agree with this—"there is no scientifically accepted evidence that strong emotional memories (or any memories for that
matter) can be repressed and subsequently recovered." I know you
make an important distinction between repression and suppres-
sion, but the idea that no memories can ever be repressed seems to
deny the existence of the unconscious. Do you really believe that
there's no such thing as the unconscious?*

There are two types of unconscious that people in psychiatry and
psychology discuss. One is uncontroversial, and the other is quite
controversial. For example, psychologists have no problem with
the so-called cognitive unconscious. The brain processes infor-

mation all the time outside of our awareness. So, for example, when we see a landscape, visual input strikes the two-dimensional surface of the retina, and the output of the subsequent unconscious processing is that it is converted into a three-dimensional image. The brain activity underlying this processing is not even in principle available to our consciousness. We are no more aware of this activity than we are of, say, the activity in our pancreas. This is the cognitive unconscious, and it is uncontroversial.

But this is not the unconscious that most people mean when they speak about the "unconscious mind." Most people are referring to the psychodynamic unconscious popularized by Freud. This is the postulated realm of repressed wishes, memories, motives, and so forth. It supposedly has its own intentions and possesses all the trappings of the conscious mind, except awareness itself. One goal of psychoanalysis was to convert this unconscious material to consciousness. And it is this Freudian unconscious mind that is controversial.

In Remembering Trauma *you have a fascinating discussion of Freud's once held and later retracted seduction theory, and it seems to me that in a way Freud might be seen as the progenitor and reflector of the memory recovery debate. By that I mean that his belief in and then abandonment of the seduction theory seems to me to encapsulate the entire debate between recovered memory and false memory advocates. Could you say something about this theory and its implications for this debate?*

Freud believed that children who are sexually abused in the first few years of life, and who repress the memory of the sexual abuse, are at risk for developing symptoms of hysteria—hysterical paralyses, hysterical vomiting, and so forth—when they reach puberty. And to eliminate these symptoms, one must help the patient recover the presumably repressed memories of childhood sexual abuse, and have the patient experience the bottled-up emotions and put the entire experience into words, into narrative. In fact, as historians of psychoanalysis have now convincingly shown, these patients never told Freud that they had been abused in the first place. They never recovered any repressed memories. His theory dictated that they must harbor these memories, and he inferred their presence from the patients' behavior. In any event, the therapy wasn't helping very much, and he abandoned this theory for what was to become classical psychoanalytic doctrine—that children had repressed sexual *fantasies* for the parent, the Oedipus complex, et cetera. But his early quasi-hypnotic attempts to unearth repressed memories do, indeed, bear an eerie resemblance to the so-called recovered memory therapies of recent years—1896 got replayed in 1996, so to speak. History, unfortunately, repeated itself.

After reading your book, one comes away realizing that neither the vividness of a memory nor the confidence with which it is held guarantees its accuracy.

Right.

Also that we know now that flashbulb memories are neither permanent nor immune to distortion.

Correct.

And that how adults see themselves in adulthood seems to shape how they remember their younger selves.

Yes.

And there's the astonishing idea that we can never describe in precise detail what was actually presented to us. For as soon as we experience anything, we immediately interpret and rewire it. Considering the reconstructive nature of memory, what are the implications for the issue of false and recovered memories? And how do we know we are remembering anything accurately?

Memory, even traumatic memory, does not operate like a video-tape machine. When we recall a memory, we reconstruct it from elements distributed throughout the brain. Of course, when there are permanent records of the remembered event—a literal video-tape, for example, or historical archives—we then have a sort of gold standard against which to compare the accuracy of our recollection. The fact that memory is reconstructive and not a video-tape means that memories are always "false" to some degree. Worries about "false memory syndrome," recovered memories of cannibalizing babies in satanic cults and so forth, provoked wide-spread alarm because the memories were false in their essence, not just in their details.

In your book you said something that reassured me: "Even when we garble the details about the past, we often get the essence right. Memory for the gist of many experiences is retained with essential fidelity, and this is especially true for events having personal, emotional significance."

Right. Because there you've got a little bit of an anchor in reality, so to speak. Just imagine if that were not the case. Evolutionary speculation is always a hazardous business. However, with that caveat in mind, it is tough to imagine a memory system evolving that had no fidelity to the facts at all, where the essence of important experiences was not retainable with reasonable accuracy. An organism that evolved a memory system like that surely would not survive the vicissitudes of natural selection. If our memory did not work reasonably well, we would not be here today having this conversation.

CHAPTER SEVEN

ON MEMORY, IMAGINATION,
AND THE SOUL

A CONVERSATION WITH THOMAS MOORE

> If you can't remember something,
> imagine it.
>
> Agnès Varda

ONE OF THE FASCINATING THINGS I DISCOVERED WHILE WORKING
on this book is that the Latin word *memoria* was the old term for
both memory *and* imagination. For the Renaissance Hermetic
philosopher Giordano Bruno, as Frances Yates reminds us in *The
Art of Memory*, "there is but one power and one faculty which
ranges through all the inner world of apprehension, namely the
imaginative power or the imaginative faculty which passes immediately through the gates of memory and is one with memory."
And as Yates also remarks, "The manipulation of images in memory must always to some extent involve the psyche as a whole."

In order to explore the relationships between and among
memory, imagination, and the soul, I turned to Thomas Moore,
the author of bestselling books such as *Care of the Soul, Soul
Mates*, and *The Re-enchantment of Everyday Life*, which celebrate, among other things, the notion that in caring for the soul
we should value the importance of images and imagination in
our ordinary daily life—being "in love," he suggests, is like being
"in imagination"—and that this is an art that allows the world to
reflect and reveal to us who we are and what the soul is. As a
young man, Moore lived for twelve years as a monk in the

Catholic Service Order; he is now a practicing psychotherapist and lecturer.

Thomas Moore spoke to me from his home in New Hampshire.

In The Re-enchantment of Everyday Life *you write: "I am visited once in a while by what feels like a memory of events and persons that could have no historical reality for me, but the mystery of their visitation makes me feel that life was indeed paradisiacal." Regarding this state of the paradisiacal, I immediately thought of the memory of childhood when, as Wordsworth wrote, "every common sight" seemed "apparelled in celestial light." What is your sense of this paradisiacal state?*

I think it has at least two dimensions. One—though it's a bit Freudian to put it this way—is that childhood is a form of paradise. But the memory of childhood isn't completely literal, because when you remember things that happen in childhood, the memory itself is a form of *imagining* childhood—it's an active memory. I don't think it's a record, it's not like playing a tape. It's going back and seeing it from where you are right now. What I'm trying to say is that when you think about childhood, you are capturing paradise to some extent, if in fact your own childhood had some paradise in it, and that's not true for everybody.

So that's one thing. Another is that paradise is what you might call a significant archetypal fantasy that is part of human imagining. I was recently preparing a talk on American spirituality, and I was thinking about how when you look at old maps of America sometimes America is called the *terra incognita*—the unknown land—or the *novus mundus*—the new world. And I think that there are a lot of paradise fantasies going on there about America, the land that hasn't been used yet. So that this idea of the paradise memory is, first of all, active and not just a tape, and second it's one that appears in many different contexts. I think it's awfully important to realize that you're not shut out of paradise forever, that certain experiences, like being in love or having a new home or a new job or moving to a new country, even traveling some-an bring you to paradise—even if it's not perfect and even

ly a portion of what you're experiencing—can evoke that

f paradise even if only momentarily. But even if it's very

think it's extremely important.

Your sense of the paradisiacal also suggests to me the mythic idea of our expulsion from the Garden of Eden and our concomitant separation from the All.

The story of Adam and Eve and paradise has been interpreted in many different ways over time, and I think they're probably all valid. One explanation is that we have been excluded from paradise and now we have surrendered our innocence in order to be knowing, in order to know what's going on and to be conscious of what is happening. That's probably true in some ways, but I don't think it's the whole story. Part of it is that we are also there before we have fallen, we are also *in* paradise, and we can be there in moments, as I was just saying, and I think it's awfully important to be able to go back to that place before we had experience—I'm thinking of William Blake's *Songs of Innocence* and *Songs of Experience*. I think it's possible to be in that place of innocence, it's important to almost have that flavor or aroma of innocence, to have it there even though life shows itself so much as a place of experience.

You write about having "a memory of events and persons that could have no historical reality for me," and you say that "heading toward enchantment is a return" and also that "we remember, in a Platonic sense, a mythic memory, an imagined period when things were in harmony." When you think about what you call "deep memory," are you doing so with this Platonic notion in mind?

Yes. I was thinking partly of Plato's Seventh Letter, in which he talks about knowledge as reminiscence. But as far as I understand it, he doesn't mean personal memory, a remembering of things that have happened to us personally, rather that there's a way in which we have an existence that is outside of time. I think Plato has sometimes been taken too literally about that, but within our experience there's a way in which memory takes us beyond our own personal experiences, and we remember what it's like to be a human being in the sense that we remember our roots, the basics out of which we are made. And I think that's Platonic memory— that kind of memory is really the discovery of who we are at our deepest level. And it's the basis of all my work—some of my friends call it "archetypal psychology," meaning that there's a way in which we try to connect with experiences like, let's say, love or death.

My mother recently died, and that experience is mine, it's very personal, but when I talk to people about it, I find out how universal it is. Certain experiences and certain thoughts and memories come up, and people will say to me, I've been through that and it was both a wonderful and a terrible thing and you'll probably experience it a certain way. Well, in those expressions I think they're really linking me up to a human memory of what it's like to have this experience of that loss. And the same might be true of getting married or getting sick or of so many things that we experience. There's a certain dimension to all these things that are not personal, and they are experienced as remembering: "I remember what it's like," and this is human memory, this is the memory of who I am before I have any experience. And I think that that's Plato.

Why do you think we forget our true and original selves, and how can we remember them?

That sounds like a Gnostic question. The Gnostics say that the soul comes to earth and forgets its original source, and the question for them is, How do we remember? Are there signs? The Gnostics say that sometimes we get messages. Some would say that dreams are the source of our memory, of who we essentially are. So it's a question that's been asked for millennia.

Personally, I think that the arts play a big role. I think that the real artist is in touch with dimensions of experience that transcend the personal. And when you're looking at certain art, what you're doing is looking at images of who we are in that original sense, and that's one way to recover a sense of who we are. It can't be just personal, it's got to be more than that. Art can be very useful for that. And religion, of course, also does it—in religious poetry and religious ritual and religious art. In so many ways I think it's the point of religion. The word *religion, religio,* is sometimes understood to mean "to be linked back"—it's not too far from *re-collect*—to that original person. So religion does it by trying to get us past personal issues, and I think religion is very important for that kind of memory. Religion and art are the two things that I think are most important.

And the third thing might be some sort of psychoanalysis—I don't mean that in just the Freudian sense but some kind of recollection of one's own life. Having to deal with and sort out certain life problems can connect you to the very deepest issues. In my practice as a therapist over so many years I always, with very few exceptions, have used dreams as a primary source. I'm focused not so much on what the person is telling me but rather on hearing the life stories people tell me as going way back and having a mythic quality. So I think that psychoanalysis, psychotherapy—care of the soul I call it—can be another way of reconnecting with that original self.

The psychologist James Hillman has said that if the father of therapy was Freud, its mother is Mnemosyne, goddess of memory and mother of the muses, "whose tenth invisible daughter must be Psyche [the soul]." What do you think is the relationship between memory and psyche, between the art of memory and the art of soul-making?

That's a very good question. I have spent a fair amount of time studying the Renaissance art of memory, written about so well by Frances Yates in her book *The Art of Memory.* In the Renaissance, memory was almost inseparably connected to astrology. So that when people lived in a culture where astrology was a way of life, which was up to about five hundred years ago, the stars and the planets were a source of memory. And in order to be able to connect to the soul of the world—to have a sense of memory, which was almost the same thing because they were very closely related—the Renaissance texts about astrology refer over and over again to the soul of the world, the *anima mundi*. So I think that the way to care for the soul through memory is to keep in mind the dynamics and the elements that make up life, not just human life but life itself. Astrology, alchemy—methods of that sort—were used to try to keep in mind all those things. The person I studied most, Marsilio Ficino [the fifteenth-century Renaissance magus], suggested that you ought to paint on the ceiling of your bedroom images of where the planets and their spirits were at the time of your birth so that every day when you get up, the first thing that you'd see is that image, and then you'd go out into the world and keep it in mind, which is a kind of memory—it's an art of memory—so that your experience would not be just personal but you'd have a depth of perspective, which really is what the soul is about. So the two things—the art of memory and the art of soul-making—are so closely connected that it's hard to imagine them not being so.

The Latin word memoria *designated both memory and imagination. What are your thoughts about the relationship between memory and the imagination?*

I think the question is, What is the imagination? The modern notion of it as referring to inventiveness and being clever and being able to come up with new ideas is not entirely what it is. *Imagination* means to be able to entertain images that make sense of the world and give your life a context and to be able to create that imagination that you can live in so that the world itself is not taken literally, just as *fact*. And that, I think, requires a life-long education in the imagination. Recently, I've gone back, as I do every couple of years, to the writings of Black Elk, the Sioux teacher who over and over suggests ways for his people to live in a sacred environment. And if you just start doing things in a manner that's not sacred, the whole thing falls apart. I think that's the same as imagination. To care for and maintain the soul in your experience requires religion because the soul is bigger than the self—psychology can't do it. But religion is a way of *imagining*, religion is a kind of main engine of the imagination. It's a way of sustaining and educating the imagination so that whatever we do we are always aware of the context in which we do things and the multiple levels on which we do them. So imagination, then, requires a certain kind of remembering. I think that religion is primarily an art of memory, it helps you keep in mind the larger context in which you live, and without that, your life gradually becomes secularized, which is what has happened to our society. And a secular society has no soul and cannot, I think, exist terribly long.

Aristotle said that memory belongs to the same part of the soul as imagination and consists of a collection of mental pictures from sense impressions but with a time element added. So perhaps one could say that remembering and imagining something are in a sense similar because one experiences them in the same manner. This would imply that whether something happened or didn't happen doesn't matter because that something keeps happening in either case. And this has many implications with regard to the debate about false and recovered memories. What are your thoughts on this?

During Renaissance times the Aristotelians and the Platonists were arguing about this. The Aristotelians generally said, quite literally, that the only thing that can be in our imagination is what we have in our sense experiences. And the Platonists were saying that the imagination and memory go far beyond that. So those are two ways of looking at it. But I think it's very significant whether something has happened in time or not. That doesn't mean that if something hasn't happened it isn't significant—it's significant in a different way. So I think that it's very important to determine whether an event actually occurred or not. I know that as a therapist you run into this with issues like sexual abuse—did it happen or did it not happen? It's very important to get to the answer of that question. But if it *didn't* happen and you have a person who's

dealing with that so-called memory, that's still extremely significant in that person's life. And that's a good example of how memory and imagination overlap, and it's sometimes very hard to sort
them out.

*According to some neurologists, abuse of various kinds can damage
brain tissue, and the brain is said to be permanently damaged and
"rewired" by these acts of abuse. It would seem that from a neurological point of view it does, as you say, matter whether something
has happened or not.*

I want to make an observation about what you just said. I don't
know what your intention was, but it sounded to me like what you
were saying was that because it has been shown that there is an effect of abuse on the brain therefore what I said is valid. And it's
hard for me to let that go by, because it's an interesting issue in itself, and I think it has to do with memory as well. From my point
of view, we can't let the literalists in science determine whether
what we say about memory is valid or not. Because something
happens to the brain doesn't validate memory in any way. It's a
description of a physical correlate of what goes on in our experience, but it does not validate this discussion of memory. To say
that this happens in the brain would be a materialist reduction of
what we're talking about. And I think that that kind of issue enters
so often in discussions of memory that one should be quite clear
about this.

*Today it seems that memories are increasingly being split off from
imagination and often seem to be lodged and materialized in, for
example, computers' storage and retrieval. We are continually losing our personal memories so that, as someone once said, our memory machines are now in a sense our amnesia machines. From the
point of view of imagination and the soul, isn't this a disturbing
new reality?*

In many ways it is. We decided years ago to put our children in a
Waldorf school, and one of the things they do there that I like is

to have the students do a lot of memorizing—they memorize long poems and recite them onstage to each other. Third graders might learn long plays in a foreign language that they don't know terribly well. They memorize together as a class, they memorize with their bodies, they move to help the memory. There are a lot of weaknesses in that educational system, but one of the strengths is that they really do learn how to memorize and to enjoy memorizing.

We need to exercise memory at that level, and it's something we have lost. But I don't think that having memory in our computers necessarily means that we're not going to have memory at other levels. I use the computer all the time, and I don't think it takes away from my experience of the many things in life that are rich and deep and important. But I make a big effort to make those things important in my life. So I will work on the computer for a couple of hours and then play the piano for a while. I may be memorizing a piece at the piano. I think that as a society we can go ahead with our technology, and yes, there will be some dangers of forgetting certain things and, as you said, materializing memory, but I think the two things can coexist, though I do think it's a danger. I hear my kids, when talking about mathematics, say, Well, we can do it on the calculator. They don't have to keep that in their heads. In our American educational system, we have a religious faith in computers and technology. And it's that transfer of faith to science that concerns me. It's not necessary to lose the imagination. I don't think the two can't exist together. But it's a danger and it could happen.

To sum up, what do you think are the basic connections between and among memory, imagination, and the soul, these three things that are so deep in our being?

Let me give you a piece of an answer, and that is that the imagination needs to be educated, as I said before, it needs to be stimulated. Now what the essence of the Renaissance meant was to spark the imagination in a certain direction by means of the achievements of the past. So you had these Renaissance artists and architects, the great ones and the not so great ones, going off to Rome and Venice and wandering the streets of Florence studying classical Greek and Roman images and seeing how the Greeks and Romans did it. They did not then go out and copy what they saw. They saw deeper into what was going on, and they also connected what they learned with what they knew of their own time and their own society. Paul Oscar Kristeller, who was one of the great Renaissance historians, says that the Renaissance was a revival of life *guided* by antiquity. What that means in relation to our issue here is that the imagination was trained, educated, and stimulated by memory. People went back to remember how people had done things in the past. And I think that's true for every endeavor today. You don't live just in the present, and I think that the overemphasis on the future today goes along with the loss of soul.

Put it this way: There's a spirited way of going into life and there's a soul way, and in the best of circumstances they're so close you can't tell them apart. But they do get split apart, and to focus on the future is a very spirited thing to do; honoring the past is a very soul thing to do. So I think that the soul and the imagination and memory come together at that level. I don't know what the medium is that connects them all, but it might be the education and articulation of images so that the imagination is given a great deal of richness, returning to the past and into the various levels of the past so that you don't get stuck in just one period.

In music you can see this happening over and over again. Think of the contemporary Estonian composer Arvo Pärt. What did he do? He went back to the twelfth-century French composers Léonin and Pérotin, and he found so much there. When you listen to Pärt you don't hear Léonin or Pérotin, but the memory is there, and this fresh imagination comes through his music. So what is it, is it memory or is it imagination? The two are inseparable.

CHAPTER EIGHT

The Griot — Storyteller and Remembrancer of the African Tribe

A Conversation with Judith Gleason

> Every man is a charabanc on which
> all of his ancestors ride.
>
> Ralph Waldo Emerson

SOMEONE HAS DESCRIBED A SCENE IN A DESERT VILLAGE IN Africa about twenty years ago where the chief brought out a television and a power generator, and the villagers sat in the sand and watched, totally transfixed, an episode of *Dynasty* dubbed into French.

The role of the African griot—the remembrancer and preserver of the tribe's genealogy, history, and culture—is in a parlous state as new technologies encroach on this bardic art. As people do everywhere, people in Africa now prefer television shows to the traditional stories, though in an odd twist, some TV stations present griot storytellers on an occasional basis. It is a tradition that refuses to die out. Griots still pass on the myths, epics, and collective knowledge of their people, and it is they who hold within them the wisdom of previous generations. In the words of one African proverb: "Old cooking pots make better sauce."

In their stories, praise poems, and prayers, griots habitually invoke the tribal ancestors: "You who laid the cornerstone / Receive our morning greetings." In tribal societies the first community is that of the ancestors. And they dwell everywhere. In the houses of the Fali of north-central Africa, the ancestors are present under the loft in the form of stones. Among the mountaineers of the Mandara, they inhabit the potteries and urns grouped around the yard. They are consulted, prayed to, and given offerings. And, most important, they are the progenitors of the race, who are continually reborn to become their own descendants. As Pierre Erny writes in his book *Childhood and Cosmos*, "The clan or lineage appears as a reservoir in which there are a limited number of souls, names, and roles, and the extended family is in fact only a collection of deaths and rebirths of always identical individuals." And the griots remember the stories of everybody.

One of the true remembrancers of this tradition is the writer and filmmaker Judith Gleason, a former teacher at New York University and author of remarkable books such as *Orisha: The Gods of Yorubaland*, *Oya: In Praise of an African Goddess*, and *Leaf and Bone: African Praise-Poems*. I conversed with her about the griots and their ancestors at her home in New York City.

There's a proverb from the Ijo people of Nigeria that goes, "He's of goblin ancestry who knows not whence he came." Why do you think that in African societies there seems to be this deep need and desire to remember where we came from?

It's important to know where we've come from because the only thing that makes mortality tolerable is this sense of inheritance and continuity. One way of knowing whence we came is the way in which a child is seen as being a reincarnation of its grandparents, who give the child his or her name. One recognizes the grandparents' features and behavior in the child. That isn't the whole personality, however, since the child has its own soul, but the grandparent is a large component of that. And if the child didn't look like a particular ancestor, you would ask a diviner, Who is this baby? And the rituals for the ancestors reinforce that notion. Now we, too, often say, "Oh, he looks just like somebody in the family" or "He got that from his grandfather who was quite a cutup!" I think that even we have an intuitive sense of that.

What they call "reincarnation" is what we might call "genetic in-heritance." In a sense, don't you think that these are two ways of at-tempting to explain the same thing?

In a way, yes. When we say, "She looks just like her grandmother" or "He acts just like the old man," it *is* like a genetic inheritance. And I'm fascinated by the similarities between my children and their grandparents, whom they didn't know very well. I see traits coming down. The more problematic traits are being inherited right and left by one's grandchildren—my granddaughter Mea-gan is sort of feisty acting and a little contrary. And my daughter says, "Well, you know where she got *that!*" Then again, a lot of it is culture, too—the stories that come down about our forebears.

"The apple doesn't fall far from the tree."

That's right. But what we don't seem to have are these spirits, these goblins. The goblin is a spirit, he's outside the human di-mension, therefore he knows not whence he came. There are all sorts of spiritual beings who have one foot in the other world to begin with, and they're here sometimes just to make mischief. They're born to die right away, and one is leery of them. A spirit wouldn't know whence he came because he wouldn't have that human ancestry, that genetic code. In the other world they don't observe genealogies.

You've written these powerful words: "Traditional African poetry, as it reflects notions of African personality, is a poetry of belonging. The isolation of the individual, whether attributed to man's 'fallen' state or to the prison of a cogitating ego or to estrangement inher-ent in the human condition, from an African perspective seems like madness. Psychological separateness like ours could only be re-garded as tantamount to annihilation by someone whose vital force is in continuous relation with that of a family composed of living as well as dead persons."

"Give the dead room to dance," said Wole Soyinka. I think that this sense of belonging is certainly related to memory. Take African praise poetry, for example: If you start praising a person, you link him to his ancestry—maybe he had a famous ancestor— or you can link him to an animal that seems to embody his characteristics, or you link him to the place he hails from—it's not just the river that flows by that place, it's the whole village where people may have migrated from. And this kind of memory is terribly important in this age of displacement, an age of refugees where people flee repression and violence of war. So they need to remember those origins and the people they left behind or the places they can never get back to because maybe they don't even exist anymore—the village having been absorbed by some other country. And those linkages need to be perpetuated culturally by the people and the families of these emigrants, and I think this is something we ought to be able to understand since we ourselves are an immigrant culture. Unfortunately, we seem to have lost a sense of that because we live in a celebrity culture, which isn't about linking a person to forebears, and I think that's pathetic. Memory is necessary in order to tell these family stories so that you remember things you did and places you used to live.

In a way, we ourselves, coming as we do from different parts of the world, are somewhat similar to the refugees you're talking about.

In a way that's true. Lately, in fact, I've been studying refugees. I once made a very special trip under very special circumstances to the source of the Niger River, which has its origin along the Guinean border. It was a magical three days. We had a Jeep, and it was the rainy season so the conditions on the road were horrible, but we made it. Once we got to the village that was closest to the source of the Niger, the community mobilized to help us and gave us a guide, the nomads on the way served us rice with clotted cream and a little pepper because someone told us that if you don't put pepper on clotted cream the taste would be revolting. Writing this up in retrospect, I realized that this area was more or less the same one that was overrun by refugees from war-torn Sierra Leone. Actually, I think we are all refugees and the world a refugee camp. I think that capitalism and the wars have completely dislocated the world. Yes, there have always been refugees, but the wars are getting worse and worse.

Coming back to the sense of estrangement we were talking about: We tend to think of madness as complete idiosyncrasy—just operating on your own battery with no sense of knowing what is going on around you—and that is a kind of madness. If you couldn't tell the village chief the name of your father, you'd seem a bit crazy. If you didn't *want* to tell the name of your father, then you'd seem suspicious. Who is your father? Why are you here? A resident of an African community acknowledges himself or herself as being part of a group or a clan. Even in Neolithic times they must have started this process.

It's said that the professional poet or griot thinks of himself as having inherited his voice from a predecessor or even from some divinity.

He does. He feels inspired, throwing cowries on the sand. You prayed for the voice of the bard, the famous bard of the village. Perhaps he takes you on as an apprentice. Here, along with memory, comes learning the trade. How do people in a traditional society learn to compose? They have to memorize the poetry and learn the oral traditions. And we think we can take a writers' workshop!

But we also have a poetic tradition that hearkens back to older writers.

Yes, writers feel they are part of the legacy of Walt Whitman and others. When Galway Kinnell stands up and reads Whitman, I know that the tradition is being *voiced*, and that tradition comes forward.

And Whitman himself has his own poetic ancestors.

Absolutely. In the Psalms for one. I don't feel I've ever been anointed by a bard, but I feel great gratitude to certain writers who have spoken to me through their work. For me it's someone like John Berger. Every time I pick up something by him, it's like going on a field trip, and I know that the next thing I write will be better.

So we have to create our own ancestors.

We do. In Mali, there are those who know the heroic literature, the equivalent of the Homeric epics—they start out as young kids and they have a yea-saying tradition, so that after a certain phrase or two, somebody has to be the yea sayer, and he hits a little metal instrument to punctuate it.

It's like shouting out "Olé!"

When I was recently on a peace march I thought of William Blake—the manacles of fear and the chartered streets of London, and here I was in the chartered streets of New York with those metal frames that were there for crowd control. So there we do create our own ancestors.

Blake wrote: "Hear the voice of the Bard! / Who Present, Past, & Future sees; / Whose ears have heard / The Holy Word / That walked among the ancient trees."

There you are.

We can check out a quotation in a book, but the griot is able to remember an incredible number of stories and lines from an epic. Someone interviewed a particular griot and asked him how he was able to remember so much, and he replied that he didn't remember but his guitar remembered. And he continued: "Once I start playing, I'm inspired and everything comes into my mind."

That's marvelous. You know the nervousness of trying to remember something, the panic in the frontal brain. But if you were reciting something with the guitar, the guitar would remember.

"While my guitar gently weeps."

That's beautiful. It's a kind of egoless memory, you just throw yourself into the sound of your guitar. The part of you that is remembering with it is going to bring that up. I don't have that tender relationship with my computer, though I used to with my typewriter. I felt that my typewriter would write on its own. It played Beethoven chords.

That typewriter was in touch with your ancestors.

It was. It was from *The New York Times* newsroom originally, and they threw it away and someone gave it to me—a nice old Royal Standard. And I sometimes think: Imagine all the great stories that were written on that in its heyday.

The griots pass on the myths, epics, and history of their people.

They're the bards of the oral tradition, and they're responsible for their people's culture. They say that when a griot dies it's as if a library has burned down. But they also interpret that history; it's not just a tradition that's remembered point by point without its relevance being stressed. They're not unaware of times-they-are-a-changing, and they try to make opinionated comparisons that are not too obvious.

What about our own sense of history?

I recently watched a program on public television that narrated the voices of the people who were slaves. And how it got remembered was very real because the African-American actors who read those parts were able to do so in a dialect that may not have been exactly the way the people spoke but was close to the way they were reported to have spoken. And I felt that something was really being perpetuated—a memory there that was passed on through those old people in the rocking chairs, telling it like it was, and yet we needed that intermediary, we needed Oprah and Ruby Dee to give us the living sense of what those people were saying. These were their folks, their ancestors. And I was terribly moved. I guess I'm more moved by the voice than I am by the image. I guess I think of memory in a griot way, coming through the voice.

They say that a griot must be anointed by what is called the "old speech" acquired from one's predecessor or ancestor or one's mother. As an African proverb goes: "When the mother cow is chewing the grass, the young calves watch its mouth."

The "old speech" would be like the classical *malinké* spoken at the source of the Niger where I mentioned I had visited. We sat, four of us, one night—one was the son of the chief whose clan owned the access to the river sources, and another was a schoolteacher who in a way belongs to two worlds but who loves his own history. There were no bards strumming instruments, but the language was flowing like the river, and the reminiscing branched into tributaries. Now, we like Shakespeare performed by the Old Vic because we feel we're really hearing him. We have a myth that when we hear John Gielgud or Laurence Olivier speak, *that* is the voice we want for Shakespeare.

That's our own old speech.

Yes. And for me, who loves the voice, that is so moving. I'm riveted by those old guys in a way that I'm not by the youngsters in Central Park who act Shakespeare in a mid-Atlantic speaking voice.

That's the "new speech."

And it doesn't go to my core. Now, James Earl Jones as King Lear had the old speech that he combined with the Shakespearean speech, and it was very rich. Paul Robeson spoke the old speech. I heard him sing with the beautiful Welsh miners' chorus, and I got gooseflesh from that. And I suppose that the ancient Greek bards maintained their old speech, too.

As you mentioned, the griot has to inherit his speech. The griot usually belongs to a caste—you followed the trade as in medieval Europe. And if you're from a griot family, you have a chance of becoming a griot—it's not necessarily true that you'll succeed, but you do have access. And you learn the prayers and partake of the libations, and there are all sorts of ceremonies to protect and cure the voice. I think they get doctored up a little bit, they go to some kind of expert in traditional medicines who gives them magical potions to rub on their bodies.

I was once very taken by a griot who was inspired by the sound of the river. And whenever he thought he was losing his memory, he would go down to the river and play his kora, that beautiful multistringed harp with its calabash resonator that rests on the stomach, and he would listen to the river going by.

Bruce Springsteen also listened to that river.

Bruce Springsteen is wonderful. He's a kind of bard for his social class. It's the workingman's tribe, and he brings that with him, and I feel it with him.

In his concerts he really creates a world of community that works against that sense of estrangement and disconnection we were talking about.

And it's a very well-grounded place to be. That is a grounded tribe. I've never been to one of his concerts, so let's both go the next time he's in town!

In a way, rock-and-roll and hip-hop are young people's bardic tradition.

I can't say I'm very experienced in hip-hop, but the other day I was in Grand Central Station handing out leaflets about an anti-war march, and I was sort of hanging out with a group of hip-hoppers, hoping that they'd come perform at the march. I really love their own little sense of community, turning their somersaults and weaving in and out of each other's bodies as they're talking, flopping around. It was great! That's the voice of the ghetto. It's different from Springsteen's, but it is also a voice of the tribe.

Actually, rock-and-roll has its own ancestry in gospel and the blues, and of course it also has its roots in Africa, and ironically, the music now returns in its own form back to Africa, where it cross-pollinates with today's music there.

Think of Taj Mahal's performances with musicians from Mali. *They're* interested in *him.*

You've written that stories in Africa are often told to a double audience—to the spirits abroad in the night and to the lively community of children.

The spirits actually listen to the stories. I love the idea that they're gathered in the trees and they're listening. Do you ever have that sense about the spirits listening, too? I suppose that in the gospel tradition and in church performances of Handel's *Messiah*, for example, the spirits are there somehow because they're summoned up. It's nice to know that they're there listening.

I've read that the Bina griot from eastern Nigeria tells his stories only at night when his melodies and words attract the night people and the witches who dance as he plays the kora. But if he stops, it's thought that the spirits might hurt him, cut the strings of his instrument, or even blind him. So the griot placates them by dedicating his first melody to them and later offers them cola nuts and wine.

You know that there are a lot of traditions in which you don't tell stories in the daytime. You tell them at night so that the spirit world comes close—we, too, can feel that at night while sitting at a campfire telling stories. The unconscious forces listen, all the spirits inside us.

Returning to our earlier discussion about the importance of remembering the ancestors, the ethnologist James Fernandez, writing of the Fang of Gabon, states that they have "the custom of praying by reciting genealogy in which men count back up to their origins until one arrives at the founders of one's clan, 15 or 20 names in the past, and beyond them to the great gods who created the Fang and mankind." And they see the ancestors in what is called the Bwiti ceremony, in which people consume the roots of the eboka plant and fly like birds with their ancestors and return to the very primordial beginnings of things. Like our return to Adam and Eve.

Is that really our primordial story? I don't know, I feel alienated from Adam and Eve somehow. I can pick up again with Ecclesiastes. But you do want to return to that primordial beginning, and I think that the strong epic traditions usually do go back through all the names of the heroes to that initial place where darkness is somehow set alight. Do we get that far back with *our* bards: Whitman or Shakespeare or Springsteen?

James Fernandez writes that after partaking of the eboka root, which is a hallucinogen, the initiate of the Bwiti cult escapes his corporeal reality, becomes light as a bird, sees his dead, and flies high above the crowds of those who have not had the fortune to know eboka. He goes beyond the village of the dead and passes great rivers or crossroads and sometimes changes color as he comes into contact with the great gods.

What an experience! Fernandez was terribly important for me because he was the one who recommended me for the grant that first sent me off to Africa, and if he hadn't lobbied for that I wouldn't have been who I am today, so I'm terribly grateful to him and think he did a marvelous piece of work with the Fang. I always used to tease him by asking how much of the eboka had he taken and what had he seen. But he did his writing before the era in which people do what they call "intersubjective ethnology" — you could call it *"intra*subjective" because it's actually taking part in and personally experiencing, in this case the effects of eboka, while also paying attention and writing about this experience. This is what we do now. Because in the past, Jim Fernandez could never have recounted in his writings his personal experiences when he took the eboka. But if he were writing it today he could.

Do you think that either you or he would be able to fly back to your ancestors?

Someone who *would* fly back is Robert Farris Thompson [author of books including *African Art in Motion* and *Flash of the Spirit*], who went to the Congo and who, upon being initiated during one of the rites, had special drops put into his eyes so that he could *see*, and later on an ophthalmologist told him that could have blinded him. He saw spirits. He wouldn't mind telling you how it was for him. He once told me what it was like to be lying in a Pygmy hut as the women were singing their beautiful choral music, which has an influence on the Fang, too, and he just said that he was in a different world.

Would one see one's own ancestors or those of the tribe?

I think you have dreams. We have dreams, and as a Jungian would say, whatever kind of dreams you have would be yours.

Does Jung's concept of the collective unconscious connect to this at all?

I don't go all the way along with that because I think there is so much cultural specificity there. But if I wandered into the world of the Fang, eating the sacred substance, I might say, "Yes, this is

my ancestor." And I know that the source of the Niger is *my*
source. That's what I discovered, even though it's not rational to
say this.

Could you say something about how you discovered this source?

The Touré people who live in Guinea are the ones who have the
responsibility for the *water* and the *word*, which are still linked in
this place. It's a connection that is hard to explain, but Marcel
Griaule's [*Conversations with*] *Ogotemmeli*—his great book on
the Dogon—is saturated with it. Words and water both are fertile.
They bring the entire world into being. The Master of the Word
is a water spirit who rises to the sun and descends as rain. In order
to be a priest of the source and go to the source, you have to be a
Touré. When I was there, the priest of the water was gone. So
when we got up to the top, the son of the earth masters was running things, and he told me that beyond this frontier was a barricade of bamboos—they looked like organ pipes—and he said that
beyond that barricade we blacks could not go, one had to be
white in order to do it, and I would have to find the source myself.
So off I went and walked along, looking for shiny sand, anything
that would give me an idea of something wet, and finally I saw a
little bit of sparkly sand, and I said, "That's it!" So I turned around
and followed that back almost on my hands and knees, trying to
discover where the water was actually gushing out of the earth.
But it wasn't gushing, it was seeping and that was it, the source of
the Niger River.

So this was your personal source as well?

I felt it was my source as well. My friend the poet Jane Cooper
wrote: "She is not at the source yet. The source is finding her
out." Which is like letting your guitar remember the music. Because I gave myself to that. What did I see there? I brought my
own tradition with me. I brought my friend Jane's words with me
and said to myself: "The source must be seeking me out, and I
will let you find me." These words came to me in what objec-

tively was a stressful situation. We had come all that way. As fate would have it, my companion had to go back to the village. I alone had to finish the mission. I had to find it, and time was of the essence. Jane's poetic words kept me from getting uptight. I relaxed in the confidence that it would happen that way. And the source *seeked* me out.

CHAPTER NINE

THE IDEA OF EMOTIONAL MEMORY
IN THE TEACHINGS OF
CONSTANTIN STANISLAVSKI

A CONVERSATION WITH ELLEN BURSTYN

And though she feels as if she's in a play,
She is anyway.

Lennon-McCartney, "Penny Lane"

CONSTANTIN STANISLAVSKI (1863–1938) IS GENERALLY ACKNOWL-edged as the twentieth century's greatest and most profound investigator of the nature and meaning of acting and the science of its mental-physical-emotional processes. Producer, director, actor, and teacher, he was the cofounder in 1897 of the Moscow Art Theater, which, rebelling against the highly artificial and mannered theater of the nineteenth century, marked the beginning of a true ensemble theater based on a realistic method of acting and production and a dramatic technique based on, in Stanislavski's words, "an unconscious creativeness through conscious technique." Under his leadership the Moscow Art Theater presented legendary premieres of, among other plays, Tolstoy's *Czar Fyodor Ivanovitch*; Chekhov's *The Seagull, Uncle Vanya, Three Sisters,* and *The Cherry Orchard*; and Gorky's *The Lower Depths.* And Stanislavski's teachings have permeated acting schools throughout the world, particularly, in the United States, the Group Theatre, the Actors Studio, and the Stella Adler Conservatory of Acting.

In his trilogy of books *An Actor Prepares, Building a Charac-*
ter, and *Creating a Role,* Stanislavski left a record of his "System"
or "Method"—an account of his theories and approaches to the
craft of acting. *An Actor Prepares* (1926) is perhaps the most influential and imaginatively conceived treatise on acting ever written, taking the form of a mock diary of a student describing and
elaborating on a series of exercises and rehearsals overseen by an
instructor whom Stanislavski calls Tortsov, who states: "An actor
must work all his life, cultivate his mind, train his talents system-
atically, develop his character; he may never despair and never re-
linquish this main purpose—to love his art with all his strength
and love it unselfishly." In *An Actor Prepares* Stanislavski dis-
cusses the attributes of a necessary and humanistic theater (and a
way of living, for that matter), among them, imagination, concentration of attention, relaxation of muscles, the super-objective,
inner motive force, faith and a sense of truth, communion, and
most important of all, emotional memory (called "Emotion
Memory" by the book's English translator, Elizabeth Reynolds
Hapgood).

In order to understand the idea of emotional memory, I spoke
to Ellen Burstyn, the distinguished leading actress of films such as
The Last Picture Show, The King of Marvin Gardens, The Exor-
cist, and *Alice Doesn't Live Here Anymore,* for which she won an
Oscar in 1975. She studied the Stanislavski technique as interpreted and developed by Lee Strasberg at the Actors Studio, has
served as its artistic director, and along with Al Pacino and Harvey
Keitel was named its copresident in 2000.

Ellen Burstyn spoke to me from her home in Los Angeles.

Stanislavski said that in the art of living a part, one basic element
is emotional memory. Someone once called emotional memories
"golden keys" that unlock some of the greatest moments in acting.
How do you yourself conceive of emotional memory?

Let's say I had a situation in a play where I had to experience, say,
grief. So if I approach it directly, trying to remember some time
when I felt grief, the emotion usually retreats, it doesn't come for-

ward so readily when called upon. But if I approach it through my senses and I, say, picture the clothes I was wearing then and see if I can feel the *feel* of the clothes on my body with my fingertips and then try to remember what room I was in and where the light was coming from, where the window was, see if I can feel the light on my face, and were there any smells associated with the room, and can I re-create those smells, see if I can smell what I smelled that day . . . and go through all of the senses — everything I saw, everything I heard, was there music playing, were there voices, and see if I can really hear them — then as I create all of those various sense memories, the emotional memory will follow. It's a question of creating all of the memories of the senses first, and then the emotional memory comes out of that.

Lee Strasberg said never to use anything that was less than seven years old. It had to be a memory that was at least seven years old in order for it to be reliable, *reliable* meaning that you can count on it every time. And it seems to be that the furthest memories have the most impact. I don't know why that is, but I know that for myself when I use something to produce a certain effect in me, if I can remember something from my childhood it's much more effective and reliable than if I remember something recent. When you've had more experiences and you've seen more things, you become a little less sensitive than you are when you're very young. Also, it's a matter of how long it's been in the memory.

You know, memories are in different parts of the body. A friend of mine who's a pianist says that the memory of a pianist is in his hands. He once said to me, "Would you like me to play the Prokofiev for you? I've got it in my hands right now." And I once had some work done on my body by a guy who did a particular kind of massaging of the skin, a rolling technique. And when it would especially hurt he would be able to tell what the emotion was by where it was in the body because different emotions are trapped in different parts of the body. Sometimes he would work on a certain part of my body and an emotion would come up. Like the fear of not getting enough of something is in the chest.

So emotional memory is a very interesting thing—it's in the body, it's in the psyche, it's in the brain, it's held in different ways and in different places.

When Stanislavski was asked what stimuli could capture emotional memory, he mentioned that a thought could do it, a familiar object, the text of the play, the stage set, and then said something similar to what you were just saying, commenting that "another important form of stimulation of emotion is true physical action and your belief in it."

I'm not sure what he means by "true physical action." For instance, if I were, let's say, sweeping the floor when somebody ran in and said, Your dog was just killed on the street outside, and then later if I started making the motions of sweeping the floor, created the sense memory of my body sweeping the floor, would that bring me to that place where I received that information? Maybe. It's always a bit elusive, you don't always know what's going to work. Usually actors try different things, and suddenly something will have a spark in it.

If we allow our emotional memories to disappear, we eventually lose touch with ourselves. But people often try to repress unpleasant and traumatic memories, and besides, doesn't attempting to contact painful memories sometimes deeply upset an actor to the point where it undermines his or her ability to create a character?

I haven't had that experience. As a matter of fact, there is some great jubilation in being able to use those old painful memories and put them to work and have them produce an effect that's like a transformation of energy. You lose old pain for new art. I've never had the experience where using emotion memory was anything but joyful. I mean *after the fact*—not at the time you're experiencing the pain, but you're also aware that you're putting it to work and the feeling afterwards is joyful. That's how it is for me anyway.

What you're saying is perhaps similar to what Stanislavski meant when he said, "Time is a splendid filter for our remembered feelings—besides it is a great artist. It not only purifies, it also transmutes even painfully realistic memories into poetry."

That's exactly it.

But surely there are persons who have had a difficult time reliving a traumatic memory, just as they might in therapy, for instance?

Oh, yes. Sure. But I don't know anybody who has tried to use his or her emotional memory in their work and then not been able to do the work because the emotional memory was so devastating. I was talking to a young actor the other day who is just new to this work, and in class he uses the emotion and it all works fine, but then the next day in his room he finds himself sitting there and weeping. And he asked, What do you do about that?

What did you tell him?

First of all, I advised him to welcome it—that you've got all those feelings, that's wonderful, that's something to be grateful for, to be in touch with them. And second, to find some kind of ritual to help him to let go. Thank the feelings. Or light a candle or whatever the ritual is for you. For instance, I sometimes will do a ritual on New Year's Eve, writing down things I want to let go of for the year and tossing them into the ocean. But I like people to make up their own rituals, however they want to do it: something that formalizes it, the gratitude to the feeling and then the release of it.

Stanislavski wrote that "we use not only our own past emotions as creative material but we use feelings that we have had in sympathizing with the emotions of others. So we must study other people and get as close to them emotionally as we can, until sympathy for them is transformed into feelings of our own." I think he may have been referring there to an actor's sympathizing with the emotional feelings of the other actors he or she is working with.

I think it's compassion he's talking about. Compassion is your ability to put yourself in another person's position and to feel what they feel. And that's basically what actors do. They step into the shoes of the character and feel what the character is feeling. I've always said to young actors that acting is an act of compassion. You feel the character—the character can't feel for himself—you feel for him.

Neuroscientists have pointed out that memories are imperfect reconstructions of our experiences. We remember how we have experienced the events themselves, remembering the remembering of something. It's even said that the act of remembering creates a brand-new memory of that memory. How does this apply to the concept of emotional memory? Is it that the feeling is more important than the exact recalling of the event that produced that feeling?

Yes, probably. There's a wonderful book called *A General Theory of Love* by three psychiatrists—Thomas Lewis, Fari Amini, and Richard Lannon—and it's about how we perceive and about what goes on in the brain. And one of the things it suggests is that if I look at something or a particular event happens and my brain records it in a particular shape, then if the next thing occurs that is *almost* like it but not quite, I'll trim off the edges where it's different. That's how we create our own world. We keep on shaping things to our expectations, to our previous experience. So when something happens—and I see this with my friends—it will be like *Rashomon*, everyone has their own version of things, and it's because in the moment that they're receiving an impression they're shaping it to fit the shape in their brain of what happened in the past. So who knows what the event itself is? It's our memory of it, and our memory is what's laid down in our brain.

I wanted to ask you about the relationship between imagination and memory. Stanislavski talks about the importance of "imagin-

ing emotions," saying that imagination can be a stimulus for one's emotional memories, and he further states: "On the stage, everything must be real in the imaginative life of the actor."

Well, for instance in the example I first gave of a sense memory where I'm creating all the different senses: I'm using my imagination when I said that there was a window on the left, and the sun was coming in the window. Now, I'm using imagination when I picture that, I'm using my imagination when I say the sun is landing on my left cheek—and right now as I'm talking to you, I actually do feel that my left cheek is feeling a little *warmer*—that becomes real then, as opposed to just the *thought* that the left cheek is warmer from the sun coming in the window. Do you see what I mean? That's the work, that's what you do. When I say that I try to remember the skirt I was wearing and it was a brown wool skirt, and now with my fingers I try to feel the texture of the wool . . . it's a little rough . . . yes, I can feel it there, a little on the surface of my fingertips, I can kind of feel the roughness of the wool. I'm actually creating a sensory feeling in my fingers, and then it becomes real. The other way is just to say: I was wearing a brown wool skirt and it felt kind of rough. That's an *idea*, that's still a thought. But when I activate the memory on my fingertips with the visualization of that skirt and try to actually feel something there and I really begin to perceive something on my fingertips—oh, it's actually warmer now—you see I'm doing it as I talk to you, and my fingertips have actually gotten a little warmer, the wool is warmer. So then it becomes real.

Stanislavski says that "our feelings are more important than our calculation." But at the same time he says that "exploring one's emotions is a first step to conscious performance." Do you think of this as a paradox?

Not at all. Lee Strasberg used to talk about how we are our own instrument. When the pianist sits down to play the piano, the piano is tuned and he plays it, that's all, that's the music. The piano doesn't get in a bad mood one day: if it's tuned, it's tuned.

But the actor can say, All right, at this moment I'm happy . . . but my mother is dying, I'm not happy, my mood is affecting me. So I strike the note on the piano which is myself and the note doesn't play. In order to tune up our own instrument and to keep it in tune such that it responds when we try to play on it, we have to *know* our emotions, know how to access them, and then become conscious of what we have to do to ourselves to make those emotions alive in us in the moment for the play.

This brings me directly to a puzzling quotation by Stanislavski. We all know about the power of Now. But Stanislavski writes: "Momentariness can never become eternal. It lives only for today, and tomorrow it will be forgotten. That is why an eternal work of art can have nothing in common with what is momentary, no matter how gifted the actors who may try to inject it."

He's of course talking about the stage, he's not talking about the momentariness becoming recorded on film. But of course with a film that wouldn't be for all eternity, it would be for the length of the film. But I'm not quite sure that I understand what he's saying. I know that the difference between good and bad acting is that good acting means being in the moment and being alive for that moment. And bad acting is when you're trying to be alive in some *other* moment, like that great moment you had yesterday when you did this in rehearsal, that was really good, let's see if I can do that. Well, it's gone, forget it, because you're not in the moment. I pick up this teacup *right now* and that's all I'm doing, I'm picking up the teacup, not: I'm trying to pick up the teacup the way I picked it up yesterday or the way I *hope* to pick it up, I'm just picking up the teacup. That's momentariness.

I've read that some actors have criticized and questioned the idea of emotional memory. Are you aware that it's sometimes thought of as a controversial concept?

I remember reading a quote one time by Liv Ullmann, and she said that she disapproved of using her own experience in acting, because if she used her own experience in acting what would she have that was for herself? And I know there are people who have that point of view. But I don't.

Some persons have criticized some of Lee Strasberg's interpretations of the teachings of Stanislavski.

Stanislavski came to America in the 1920s, and many people met him and were deeply impressed by him, including Lee and Stella Adler. But Stella and Lee had a disagreement about the issue of the idea of "as-if." Stella thought that you didn't have the emotion, it was "as if" you did. The fact of the matter is that I studied with both of them, and they're both right. Sometimes one thing works and sometimes another. And I never understood any reason for either of them to have a point of view that excluded the other one. It's always surprising—sometimes something will pop up that you never expected. And you'll find yourself working in a different way than you had before, and it's very mysterious and all-inclusive. So I've never quite understood the reason for the controversy.

Speaking of the concept of "as-if," the director Peter Brook once wrote: "In everyday life, if is a fiction; in the theater, if is an experiment. In everyday life, if is an evasion; in the theater, if is the truth. When we are persuaded to believe in the truth, then the theater and life are one." So "as if" and "is" can sometimes come together.

Isn't that great. Yes, because you can *do* the as-if—it's "as if" I'm sweeping the floor with a broom but I don't have a broom. But then if my belief in my real physical action is full enough, then it *is* a broom and I am sweeping. And what was "as-if-I'm-sweeping" becomes "I-am-sweeping." That's when the *if* becomes the *is*.

Stanislavski writes: "Our time of creativeness is the conception and birth of a new being—the person in the part. It has a natural act similar to the birth of a human being." And although it must seem obvious, when I read An Actor Prepares, *playing a part and living one's own life seem to be the same, as if we're all in a play.*

That's right. I always say that acting is my spiritual path because when you learn how to be in the moment in life, then you go on-stage and it's blown away because there are people out there watching you as a witness, and suddenly you care about what the witness thinks. So all of your being in the moment offstage now suddenly is blown away, and you have to recollect yourself and re-center your focus so that you're in the moment now and onstage despite the fact that you're being watched. So it's the same process but in another context. But as you learn one, you learn the other.

The notion that we live in a play or a dream reminds me of the state called lucid dreaming, in which a person can train himself to be aware that he's dreaming in his dream.

I've never been able to do that. But sometimes I will be in life, and I will see it as a play. I will see it as if there's an unseen direc-tor directing me. You know, you have those reality jumps where you're inside your head and you're looking out your eyes, you're doing whatever you're doing, then all of a sudden you jump out of that and witness yourself doing it. Well, it's that feeling when you are the witness, you're seeing yourself in the play of your life.

Stanislavski gives the following instruction: "Close your eyes and ears, be silent, and try to discover with whom you are in mental communication. Try to find one single second when you are not in some contact with some object." Isn't this the same process that one might experience while meditating?

Of course. But it's all about that. That's what he means by "con-scious acting." It's really what my spiritual teacher Hazrat Inayat Khan means when he talks about mastery as being in control of all of the details. And mastery in life means being in control of all the details, and mastery on the stage is the same thing.

CHAPTER TEN

REMEMBRANCE IN THE JEWISH TRADITION

A CONVERSATION WITH LAWRENCE KUSHNER

> Remembrance is the secret of redemption.
> Forgetfulness leads to exile.
>
> Baal Shem Tov

THE HEBREW WORD ZAKHOR—MEANING "REMEMBER"—IS AN IN-junction and commandment. According to Yosef Yerushalmi, the verb *zakhor* appears 169 times in the Bible, usually referring to Israel or God as the subject ("Remember now thy Creator in the days of thy youth"—Ecclesiastes). The Bible also proposes a reciprocal relationship such that if *you* remember God, God will remember *you* ("Go and assemble the elders of Israel and say to them: The Lord, the God of your fathers, the God of Abraham, Isaac, and Jacob has appeared to me and said: I have surely remembered you"—Exodus). Conversely, in the Bible there is also the minatory fear that God may forget you ("The Lord has forsaken me; my God has forgotten me"—Isaiah, an entreaty foreshadowing Jesus' stricken cry from the cross). And then there is God's own fear that *He* will be forgotten ("O Israel, never forget me"—Isaiah), suggesting the old rabbinic notion that God himself is in exile, that man and God are collaborators in each other's destiny, and that God requires man to redeem Him from exile. The act of memory is an imperative for this redemption.

Why in the Jewish tradition is there such an intense desire to remember? Throughout history collective memories were important to fortify the identity of a persecuted and dispersed people. However, there is a decline of Jewish collective memory, and there is an ambivalence with regard to the nostalgia for the past and sense of rejection of that past that many Jews feel today. As Hans Meyerhoff has written, "Previous generations *knew* much less about the past than we do, but perhaps *felt* a much greater sense of identity and continuity with it."

One of those who has profoundly connected the Jewish past and present is Lawrence Kushner, rabbi for thirty years of Congregation Beth El in Sudbury, Massachusetts, and currently the Emanu-El Scholar at the Congregation Emanu-El in San Francisco. In lucid and inspired books such as *The Book of Letters: A Mystical Alef-bait*, *The River of Light*, *Honey from the Rock*, *Invisible Lines of Connection*, and *The Way into Jewish Mystical Tradition*, Kushner has explored and meditated on the seemingly unfathomable realms of the Jewish mystical tradition, explaining, enriching, and renewing it for our own time.

Lawrence Kushner spoke to me from his home in San Francisco.

What are some of your immediate thoughts about the idea of remembering in the Jewish tradition?

Let me start with the Siddur, the Jewish prayer book, in which at the end of the morning liturgy there's something called *Shesh Z'chirot*, which means "six things to remember." There are six things that we are commanded to remember in the Torah. And it is a very interesting list. The first one is to remember the going out from Egypt; the second is to remember the Sabbath day; the third is to remember standing at Sinai; the fourth is to remember the way our parents tried God in the wilderness—"remember and never forget how you provoked the Lord your God in anger in the wilderness"; the fifth is to remember what God did to Miriam, the sister of Moses, on the journey out of Egypt—she was afflicted with leprosy, apparently for badmouthing Moses, who had married a Cushite woman; and the sixth is to remember Amalek. [The Amalekites were a marauding Negev tribe and the paradigm enemy of Israel.] And this last one is the most fascinating from the point of view of memory because the commandment literally says: "You shall blot out the memory of Amalek from under heaven. Do not forget." It's a double whammy loop: "Remember it; forget it. Remember it; forget it." So there are six times when the word *remember* is used, and they do comprise a fascinating list, and the mind just begs to find the pattern.

What fascinates me is that somebody would bother to put them in a prayer book. Remember Egypt, remember Shabbos—that's easy; remember Sinai—a piece of cake. But number four—remember how your parents were obnoxious in the wilderness—that's not considered to be high Judaism. Quoting it, it says: "Remember your parents' waywardness, your obstinacy"—that's the kind of thing we like to repress and forget. There are more terrible things to remember, and that injunction is a very subtle thing to remember.

As for the injunction about Miriam, I don't know what that's doing there. Of all the things to remember that God did—I mean, there are people who did worse things and to whom God did more dramatic things, so why that injunction? I just don't know. And the last commandment, to remember Amalek, is very important. It has to do with remembering what your enemies did to you. What's fascinating about that is that it seems to be a violation of the commandment which says that you shouldn't remember the bad that people did to you because that would constitute bearing a grudge. According to the Talmud, if you even remember that somebody hurt you, your job is to go to that person, tell him that he hurt your feelings, and if he apologizes accept his apology and forget it. And if he doesn't, well, it's then his problem, it's not yours, you've got to get on with your life. So the injunction about Amalek poses an interesting problem: that we should remember our enemy so that we can blot out his name. It sort of hits you on both sides of the jaw at the same time.

What else do you think about concerning the Jewish sense of memory?

Judaism never portrays itself as young, it always portrays itself as an old man who remembers everything. To make the point, when was the last time you saw a picture or a painting of a young Jew? No such thing. It's always an old Jew, whose face is wrinkled by what he remembers. Christianity has infants, but there are no pictures of Jewish infants. When you see pictures and photos in the tourist shops in Israel, it's generally those depicting old Jews. We have reverence for age and the wisdom that comes with it. It's interesting to remember Franz Rosenzweig's idea that the old man conducting the Passover seder is indistinguishable from the four-year-old grandchild sitting across from him at the table.

Why do you think there's such a strong need to remember in the Jewish tradition?

I'm uncomfortable with making that a basic tenet of our teaching. Because it seems to me that any healthy religion is going to have memory as a central gesture. It feels a bit too chauvinistic for my comfort to claim that only we Jews remember things. Everybody remembers stuff. It's more instructive to ask what do Jews *do* with memory.

What do you think Judaism does with it?

Well, we reenact things. What happened was—and this is an insight of the great scholar of Jewish mysticism Gershom Scholem—that a lot of Jewish holidays and ceremonies were originally mythic, and by mythic I mean that they celebrated events that were eternally recurring and circular. In pagan religions God dies and is reborn and it happens every year at the same time. But Scholem points out that Judaism took these mythical celebrations that were originally agrarian (which is why they were circular and annual) and made them historical. Living in the bounty of the harvest at Sukkot, for example, became a memory of our wandering in the wilderness, where we lived in huts. And on Passover the celebration of the first spring lamb and the first sheaf of barley, which happened every year, became a commemoration of our redemption from Egypt. And Shavuot, the festival of weeks, came to commemorate the receiving of the Torah. Now the festivals celebrate historical events. And the important thing about historical events is that they are unrepeatable; history is linear, not circular. And therefore history is not repeatable, each day brings with it an obligation and an urgency. In pagan religion there is an attitude of, Well, if we don't do it right this year we'll do it right next year or the one after that. It's relaxed. But Judaism is more urgent because there will never be a tomorrow that's like today; what is available for us to do today will never be available again. Dr. Daniel Matt, a personal friend and a translator of the *Zohar* [*Book of Splendor*], once shared with me an amazing *responsa*, a formal reply to a legal question. Jews would write letters to their rabbis, and the rabbi might forward the queries to the ranking doyen of the generation, and the answers would acquire the status of a legal precedent. Apparently, some sultan in celebration of his birthday announced that everyone who was in his jail would be permitted to be free for one day and the prisoner could pick which day. And some guy actually wrote his rabbi asking which day he should pick. Should he go free on Purim, which celebrates salvation from our enemies, or should he go free on Passover, which celebrates the redemption of Egypt? Or should he do it on Hanukkah or Yom Kippur? And the rabbi writes back, effectively saying, "Schmuck, do it today!" I mean: Today is it; there is no tomorrow. So Judaism as a religion of linear history and nonrepeatable events remembers the past with an often bittersweet feeling because of what we could have done but didn't. The window of the past is forever closed. We have this same theme at the conclusion of Yom Kippur, when we say that the gates are closing and that once the gate is closed it doesn't open again. Prayers that could have been offered, deeds that could have been done, words that could have been spoken — that day will be forever gone.

Yosef Yerushalmi writes that if Herodotus was the father of history, the fathers of meaning in history were the Jews, and for the Jews

God seems to be known only insofar as He reveals Himself histori-cally.

In *The Prophets*, Abraham Heschel talks about the prophets bringing a whole new dimension to the idea of meaning in history. He says that God and Jews talk to one another through the nonrepeatable events of history. So we have a sense of prophetic urgency and the importance of action. I would say that the expulsion from the Garden of Eden began history. Prior to that nobody had calendars or watches, and after that everything is recorded and remembered.

You've written that "leaving the garden is a metaphor for our forget-ting that we are one with the universe. Holy awareness is the only way to return." What is the connection between the act of becoming aware and remembering?

Let me take half a step back. One of my colleagues, Rabbi Ne-hemia Polen, an Orthodox rabbi in Boston, says that because God has infinite awareness, God cannot remember anything or dream anything because, for God, there is no past or future. To enter that mode of mystical awareness is to swallow all time. Then Eden means an unimpeded, undifferentiated presence within the divine, flowing, infinite consciousness. After that, history be-gins and you start remembering what you don't have anymore and yearn to go back. I suspect that the only way to go back is through *unio mystica*, the mystic moment, loss of the self's boundaries, dissolution into the divine timelessness. A novel I'm just finishing begins with the following quotation: "Time is just God's way of making sure that everything doesn't happen all at once." That's by George Carlin.

The comedian?

Yes. I think it's brilliant.

So we leave the garden and our sense of primordial unity and then forget that we are one with the universe.

That's right. Because now, at this moment, I think you're different from me. I think you're in New York and I'm in San Francisco and that yesterday we spoke on the phone and are talking again now. . . . But this separateness, this otherness, from a mystical point of view is illusory. When we're back inside that divine presence, we have no need for memory because there is no past, no history (and no future), only an eternal present.

In the Passover Haggadah it says that in every generation each person should regard him- or herself as if he or she personally had come forth from Egypt. I had a congregant who once took a geography course at the local high school, and they asked if anyone had been to Egypt and she raised her hand and replied, "Yes, every year for about an hour!"

In your book Honey from the Rock *you write: "Judaism focuses on the point where the two worlds [this world and the other world] meet: Sinai. And the inscrutable record of that encounter: Torah. We seem to gain our invitation to the holy world by virtue of our presence there at that awesome mountain. Because the Jew is a member of a community who was present when the other world flooded this one with meaning, we are able to return as often as we wish, simply by remembering."*

Think of the Torah as a postcard we've written to ourselves to be read at some later time when we've forgotten what it was like at Sinai. The Torah is a mnemonic device; whenever I read it, Sinai comes alive again. It's like looking through the pages of a photo album: Oh, I remember that summer when we lived at that house and we did this and that and it was so beautiful and now it comes back to me. And if that family album happens to record the most meaningful event in history, then it becomes that much more holy.

Steve Thomas in his book *The Last Navigator: A Young Man, an Ancient Mariner, the Secret of the Sea* tries to find out how the ancient Polynesians were able to navigate the Pacific without instruments. He befriends a man named Piailug, who was the last navigator: "There was no powerful mathematical model that one could apply as in western navigation, nor were there primers and instruction books in case one forgot something. Piailug had only his senses and his memory. So critical was memory to navigation that it defined his notion of courage. Piailug said to me, 'To navigate you must be brave and to be brave you must remember. If I am brave it is because I remember the words of my fathers.'"

There's another amazing story by the Hasidic Rabbi Nachman of Bratslav called "The Seven Beggars." The scene is a memory competition regarding the Garden of Eden. The contestants vie to see who has the earliest memory. One remembers "when they cut the apple from the branch." Another remembers "when the fruit first began to be formed." Still another remembers "the taste before it enters the fruit." Finally, the blind beggar, who is telling the story, says, "I was yet a child, but I was there too, I remember all these events, I also remember nothing." And they answered, "This is indeed an older memory than all." How does one remember nothing?

There are two primary Hebrew words which Jewish mysticism elevates to cosmic ontological status. The first is *yesh*, which means "something." But it means more than just material "something"; it means "everything" and "anything"—material, emotional, even spiritual—that has a border, a boundary, a beginning, an end, a definition. And the vast majority of the time we inhabit the world of *yesh*. *Yesh* is inescapable. *Yesh* is bad only if you think that that is all there is. Because beyond and beneath *yesh* is another order of being, and it is *ayin*, which means "Nothing" with a capital N. *Ayin* does not mean "zip" or "nothing" (with a lowercase *n*) or "bupkes" (which, by the way, literally means "small goat droppings"!). *Ayin* has no beginning and no end, no boundary, no border, no definition. You probably can't say as much about it as we've just said. It is the mother lode of being, the root stratum of existence. It is the ocean, and all *yesh* are waves of that ocean. And when the blind beggar says, "I remember Nothing," what I think he's saying is, "I remember the infinite, the eternal; I remember God; I remember the source from which all being comes." In other words, by the way you pick up a fork, by the way you hold a pen, by the way you hold your lover, by any deed that you do, you potentially can raise it and yourself to the order of *ayin*, to boundlessness. You effectively take something and turn it back into Nothing! What makes all this so fascinating is that we're playing with this shift back and forth between a world in which time is essential and a world of timelessness, in which memory is dissolved into an eternal present.

The philosopher Avishai Margalit in his book The Ethics of Memory *writes about how in the Jewish tradition one distinguishes between forgiveness and forgetting. And he quotes God's words from Jeremiah: "For I will forgive their wrongdoing and remember their sin no more," and Margalit says that while God forgets what He has forgiven, we forgive but do not forget.*

I like it and I don't like it. Jews are stuck with this notion—and this goes back to the Amalek quote—that you've got to remember what people did to you, otherwise they can do it again. But you have to put that together with what I think is the need of a person who, for example, has been abused to forget everything, because if you go on remembering it, it goes on abusing you. Unfortunately you see that in a lot of Jews today. Personally I have turned down several VIP tours of the Holocaust Museum in Washington because I don't want to remember, and I don't think I want the world to waste time remembering me as a victim either. I want to remember its horror only to make sure that such a thing never happens to me or to anyone else ever again. I wish I had a different obligation, but you don't get to select your memories. If I was abused, I was abused. The trick (perhaps as with the Amalek commandment) is only to figure out a way to keep it in consciousness enough so that it doesn't happen again but then forget it. The best thing for someone who has been through something horrific is to get on with it. I mean, what good does it do you?

But what about George Santayana's famous remark that he who doesn't remember the past . . .

. . . is condemned to repeat it. And I can see that that is a wise thing. I guess I'm thinking that there are two kinds of forgetting. There's a kind of forgetting where something is totally gone and you have no recollection of it, and there's a kind of forgetting such that it's out of consciousness but there's an alarm that goes off whenever the conditions obtain that can lead to it happening again.

Let's say I walk down a dark alley and get mugged. Remembering I got mugged serves me no useful purpose. But I don't want to forget it entirely. I want to have some psychic mechanism so that the next time I'm walking down the street and want to cut through a dark alley, all of a sudden a bell starts ringing and says: No, no, remember. I'm not going down this alley, I'll take a different route. And then I forget it again.

Obviously with the Holocaust the Jews have learned a horrible lesson about what it means to be victimized by the full power of a technocratic state gone mad. But I would argue that we seem to have forgotten how to help other people who are suffering it now.

In my former congregation I helped form a group whose subject was "Jews Against Genocide," but the name of the group was If Not Us, Who? And that's how I would respond to a Holocaust memory. I'm not interested in looking at pictures of a gas chamber. I'm interested in looking at pictures of Rwanda or other places where genocidal things are occurring right now. I know about that in my gut as a Jew, so therefore that places a unique obligation on me—that's the part I don't want to forget.

CHAPTER ELEVEN

Divine Remembrance
in the Sufi Tradition

A Conversation with Robert Frager

Will you, won't you, will you, won't you,
  will you join the dance?
Will you, won't you, will you, won't you,
  won't you join the dance?

Lewis Carroll,
"The Lobster Quadrille,"
in *Alice's Adventures in Wonderland*

Sufism is the thousand-year-old mystical heart of Islam. But the essential truths of Sufism are manifest in the mystical core of all religions. As the Sufi poet Rumi says, "There are hundreds of ways to kneel and kiss the ground." People designate the Infinite or the cosmic source of all things as God or Allah or Yahweh or Brahman or the Tao or, as the Sufis do, the Beloved. And those who kiss the ground desire nothing less than to empty themselves of the illusory sense of separateness, self-boundaries, and self-constructions; the distinctions, classifications, comparisons, and discriminations of knowledge; and the alienating sense of everyday consciousness in order to embrace the unmediated experience of the union with the Divine. As the tenth-century poet Sheikh Abu-Saeed Abil-Kheir, having experienced this union, said of himself: "Under this cloak is nothing but God. Introduce me as 'Nobody, Son of Nobody.'"

The secret in Sufism is the remembrance of God and the opening of the heart to divine love. As the Sufi Sheikh Muzaffer

Ozak has written: "Love makes us speak; love makes us moan; love makes us die; love brings us to life; love makes us drunk and bewildered; it sometimes makes one a king. Whichever direction the lover takes, Lover and beloved, rememberer and remembered, are ever in each other's company, always together."

Rumi, as rendered by Coleman Barks, puts it this way:

I was dead, then alive.
Weeping, then laughing.

The power of love came into me,
and I became fierce like a lion,
then tender like the evening star.

He said, "You're not mad enough.
You don't belong in this house."

I went wild and had to be tied up.
He said, "Still not wild enough
to stay with us!"

I broke through another layer
into joyfulness.

He said, "It is not enough."
I died.

Robert Frager is a practicing psychologist and founding president of the Institute of Transpersonal Psychology in Palo Alto, California. He is also a Sufi sheikh (spiritual guide) and is known to his thirty or so student dervishes (a dervish is someone who is an initiate in a Sufi order), with whom he meets three times a week at his Redwood City, California, branch of the Turkish-based Halveti-Jerrahi Order, as Sheikh Ragip. "The people I work with," he says, "really feel like a family. I feel they're my sons and daughters. Which is wonderful. It's a blessing like nothing else." In the words of his previously mentioned teacher Sheikh Muzaffer, "The sheikhs are the pourers of the wine and the dervish is the glass. Love is the wine."

Both psychologist and sheikh, Frager is the coeditor of *Essential Sufism*, a marvelous collection of stories, poems, aphorisms, and fables from all eras of Sufism, from thousand-year-old prayers to contemporary writings; and the author of a truly life-changing book, *Heart, Self, and Soul: The Sufi Psychology of Growth, Balance, and Harmony*, the first work by a Western psychologist to explore the Sufi tradition as a path of psychological insight and self-transformation.

Robert Frager/Sheikh Ragip spoke to me from his home in Los Altos, California, about the idea of Divine Remembrance in Sufi thought and practice.

In your book Heart, Self, and Soul, *you write about the Sufi template of our being as consisting of our physical and psychological functioning and of our spiritual nature, which is the human soul, the secret soul, and the secret of secrets. Could you say something about the secret soul, which you say is the part of us that remembers God, and its connection to the Sufi idea of Divine Remembrance?*

This system is one I really learned orally from my own teachers, but there are other versions of it—Aristotle also had a version of the different souls, for example. This system is based on an evolutionary premise: that we move from the mineral to the vegetable and to the animal souls. After the animal soul, there's the personal soul, which is rooted in the brain. All human beings have this, but it's not completely unique to humans; higher mammals also display fairly complex cognitive functions, though not as complex as ours.

What separates us from the animals is the human soul, which involves the opening of the heart such that one begins to feel compassion or to feel love on a deeper level. That's rudimentary with animals, though it's definitely there. But at the level of the human soul, one is struggling to express more consistently this compassion and love. So in a way, it's a matter of striving. One is struggling to move to the next stage.

The secret soul is sometimes also called the angelic soul because angels are in constant prayer and remembrance; angels don't forget God. That capacity is within us as well, but we have to develop it. Angels don't develop, they stay at that level throughout their existence.

A number of my teachers have talked about this notion that as Muslims we pray five times a day and we do practices involving the remembrance of God. But the goal is to go beyond that to *constant* prayer, *constant* remembrance. And that is what is happening at the level of the secret soul, the angelic soul.

So the intention is that one should never forget God for even an instant.

There's a wonderful story of two of the great academic Muslim authorities who go to interview a saint. They say to themselves, "Well, let's see how much he understands of the Islamic law, because even saintliness must be based on a lawful, ethical daily life." So when they meet him they ask, "When do you take ablution, when do you need to cleanse yourself as preparation for prayer?" The saint tells them, "Do you mean for you or for me?" This shocks the scholars because, as they understand it, there's just one set of rules.

The saint continues: "Let me tell you about the rules for *you*." And he lists exactly what the tradition states, that you take ablution after you use the bathroom, or if you bleed—there are a whole set of rules. "We thought that was for everybody. What do you mean between you and us?" The saint replies, "For me, I need to take ablution if I ever forget God."

Beyond the secret soul, what is the secret of secrets?

The secret of secrets is the divine spark within each of us. Remembrance is remembering that which we already know. It is to get in touch with that divine spark that God has placed within each human being. In the Koran it says that God breathed from the divine soul into Adam; another way of translating that would be that God placed a divine spark into every human being. And that divine spark is the secret of secrets. My master put it this way:

That spark in us could set the whole universe on fire. It's greater than the universe itself because it's a spark of what is infinite. And it's within every one of us. Who we are is far more than who we think we are.

"To practice remembrance," you've said, "is to unveil the knowledge and power and beauty of this spark of God within us."

The Sufis would say that God is present everywhere, but there's something special about the human being in the sense that we have a special destiny and a special set of responsibilities. In the Koran it specifically says that God put that divine spark in humanity. The Jews became a chosen people by accepting a certain responsibility to follow God's law. But the Sufis would say that *all* humanity, starting with Adam, accepted that responsibility. Because of that, our whole self-image and our image of each other should be different. This is why my master once said, "It would be a sin to destroy the great holy sites on the planet, but it's a worse sin to injure any human heart. Because, after all," he said, "the Kaaba in Mecca and Solomon's temple in Jerusalem were built by human beings to honor God, but the human heart was built by God to house God."

In Heart, Self, and Soul *you mention that if we injure the hearts of those who are close to us, we damage the "divine temple" within them and that this causes our own hearts to harden and close down.*

Again, my master said: Every act we do either softens or hardens the heart. Every kind word, look, or gesture softens the heart and unveils that spark to us. But every unkind word, gesture, or look hardens the heart. And not just that: Every kindness causes a flower to bloom somewhere on earth, and every unkindness causes a thorn to grow. So everything we do has a profound effect within us and also affects the world around us.

You also say that one remedy for hard-heartedness is remembrance of God. Which brings us full circle.

The Prophet Muhammad said: "For everything that God created, God also created a polish for it. And the polish for the heart is remembrance." Remembrance can also be understood as an act of unveiling the spark, and unveiling the spark is another way of saying "softening the heart." They're really functional equivalents.

It sounds as if remembrance can be a therapeutic tool to open up the heart as well as to deal with other blocks in the human psyche.

Absolutely. I've been involved for many years with what is called "transpersonal psychology," which maintains that if you work with the whole person—the body and mind and spirit—working at any level is working on the whole system. We are fundamentally embodied spirit or embodied soul, and so any act of remembrance or any other spiritual act nourishes the whole being, and does so more profoundly than merely physical or emotional nourishment. We think that something has to be therapy to be therapeutic. So that to heal oneself psychologically one has to go to a therapist, or to heal oneself physically one has to go to an M.D. But healing the soul is therapeutic in a deeper sense.

In Arabic the word dhikr *designates both repetition and remembrance. And you've explained that remembrance of God begins with the repetitions or invocations of one of God's ninety-nine names by the tongue. Then the repetition descends from the tongue to the remembrance of the heart, and remembrance of the heart deepens and becomes the remembrance of the soul. Could you say something more about remembrance's beautiful inner journey?*

It certainly is a journey within. We begin superficially, that's where you have to start. We begin with the outer practice of remembrance, or one could say the *imitation* of remembrance by a mechanical repetition of the tongue. It's not real remembrance; we're merely imitating those who are truly in a state of remembrance. But when we continue, that practice and that imitation awaken something within us—the remembrance deepens, it goes

within, and rather than mechanical repetition, somehow the remembrance begins to come *from* us, and we begin to be engaged
in a deeper way, rather than just reciting words. And that becomes deeper still as this process goes more deeply inward, until
ideally we get in touch with that depth in us which is in remembrance or which is a state of union.

Many of the great Sufis have pointed out that in the depths of
who we are, we are already in union with God and we have
nowhere else to go. We're not going to get any better than that. So
in a sense the *dhikr* [the practice of the remembrance of God]
gets us closer and closer in touch with that deep part of us that is
in remembrance and that has never really been out of unity with
God.

Even though we think we are separate and experience separateness, there's a part of us that has never experienced separateness. In the Turkish Sufi tradition they say, First you do the *dhikr*
[remembrance], and then the *dhikr* does *you*, and eventually
there's no you and no *dhikr*.

What can you say after that?

Yes. I wish I knew what they were talking about [laughing]. I certainly understand the movement of the *dhikr* from the tongue to
the heart, that's something I have experienced. I believe I've
tasted some of that deeper movement, but I can't say I understand it.

*You've said that as the dervishes call on God, they also begin to re-
member the Divine within themselves. In Sufism implicit in the
term* remembrance *is the notion that we are coming back to what
we once knew and what we have already learned and who and what
we really are but have forgotten. The Greek word for truth,* aletheia,
literally means "no forgetting."

That's wonderful. And of course Plato taught that it *is* all within,
there's no knowledge "out there," it's all within us. I think that
when people talk about Platonic ideas, they locate them some-

where else, out in a special place outside of ourselves, but my Sufi teachers say that it is all within us. In fact, my first teacher insisted that the human being is the macrocosm and the universe is the microcosm, because what is within us is infinite, greater than the entire universe.

It sounds as if Plato were a Sufi or the Sufis were Platonists.

[Laughing] Well, certainly the great Sufi scholars read Plato and Aristotle and brought that tradition back to the West after it was lost.

You've mentioned the dhikr, *the Remembrance of God ceremony. I gather that the dervishes of most Sufi orders come together weekly to perform this ceremony, during which they attempt to unveil the Divine Face through Divine Remembrance, and that this ceremony features breath, sound, and movement. Could you say something about the Ceremony of Remembrance?*

The Ceremony of Remembrance of God is rooted in the actual experiences of the great saints in the Sufi tradition. So we're following and imitating an outer form developed by those who knew; we follow this form in order to get to that inner reality. In virtually every Sufi order the *dhikr* includes reciting some of the ninety-nine names of God—some orders do this silently, some aloud. In our order we have a daily practice that is silent and a group practice in which we recite aloud. As we recite together aloud, ideally the dervishes breathe and chant the names of God in ever deepening unison. And generally, as you're saying one of the divine names, the head moves down slightly to the left toward the heart, putting that name into the heart, putting those tiny sparks of remembrance with each repetition of God's names and *collecting* them in the heart.

My first master said that as you say the phrase *La ilaha ilallah* ["There are no gods but God"], with *La ilaha* you turn to the right, and what you're saying is "no gods," which is really saying that none of what's going on in the world is anything but tempo-

rary and ephemeral—and then when you say *ilallah*, "but God,"
you're saying that there is something eternal and real. And you're
constantly looking to the right and saying *La ilaha* ("not this,"
which is what the Hindus also say), but when we say *ilallah*
("there is God") we move our head to the left and slightly down.

My master explained this practice: The first half, the *La ilaha*,
is as though there's a temple that has gotten old and disused and
dirty because it hasn't been kept up, which is the heart of those of
us who tend to forget God and pursue a lot of worldly goals. So
we sweep the temple of the heart and begin to cleanse it, and with
ilallah we put God on the altar. We sanctify the altar. So with
each repetition we're cleaning and sanctifying the heart temple.

When most people think of movement in the dhikr, *they immediately think of whirling. Do the dervishes of your Halveti Order
whirl during the ceremony?*

The dervishes of the Mevlevi Order, which was founded by Rumi
(actually organized by his son), do whirling, but that's just one of
forty-plus major Sufi orders. The rest of us don't whirl. Whirling
is a very profound, very demanding discipline.

What we do in my order looks a little bit like Greek folk danc-
ing, where we move in a circle, and generally the left foot moves
to the left and the right foot moves slightly in back of it. As we
move, we chant, and we form a circle moving to the left, counter-
clockwise, which is, in a way, moving to the heart again, slightly
to the left of the center of the chest.

In our order we begin with seated chanting, and at a certain
point the sheikh says, "Everyone rise." In the old days the ceremony would go on for hours and hours; the sheikh would wait
until the dervishes couldn't sit still any longer, because the energy built up was so powerful that they had to move, and *then* the
dervishes would get up and circle or, quote, "dance"—but I don't
like the word *dance* because it has so many other connotations.
So you're moving from sitting and swaying and breathing and
chanting to the point when the energy builds and you stand and
move.

This reminds me of the Round Dance of Jesus, described in the Gnostic Acts of John, when Jesus, anticipating arrest, brings his followers into a circle, holding hands to dance, while he stands in the center and chants:

> I will be saved,
> And I will save. Amen.
> I will be released,
> And I will release. Amen.
> I will be wounded,
> And I will wound. Amen.
> I will be born,
> And I will bear. Amen.
> I will eat,
> And I will be eaten. Amen.

To me these circling dances suggest the idea of being at one with the universe, of surrendering in the sense of the dissolving of the "I" and the "you."

Yes, it's that false dichotomy that we're so attached to in ourselves. Most of the mystical traditions teach that the sense of the "I" eventually goes, that the dichotomy disappears at the end of the path. The last level is sometimes called the pure self. Sheikh Safer, my second Sufi master, once said very gently, "It's very hard to take the 'I' out of oneself."

The seventeenth-century German priest and poet Angelus Silesius once remarked that God can't visit a person unless the person isn't there.

That's like the word *fakir* [a person who practices Sufism]. *Fakir* means "a poor person," but it's spiritual poverty—the heart is empty so God can fill it. How can God come into a heart that's filled with other things?

The etymology of that word is fascinating. It comes from the Arab word *faqr*, which means "poverty." Some of the Sufis in

India did various practices like piercing their skin with needles or walking on broken glass when they were in certain states, when they weren't identified with themselves or their bodies. But eventually the whole thing got commercialized and became perverted, and you had *fakirs* sitting on beds of nails, walking on hot coals, performing the Indian rope trick, to show off for money. And so that word became the root of the word *faker*. So it's interesting that the initial meaning suggested someone who didn't care about *worldly* things, who was poor in his attachments to the world, and it turned into just the opposite.

Rumi once said, "Don't regret what's happened if it's in the past, let it go, don't even remember it." In Sufi thought it seems that we should not forget to remember God, but we should forget to remember the past. Why should this be?

There is an old Sufi saying, "The dervish is the child of the moment." We are supposed to live in the present because dwelling on the past or the future can be tremendously unproductive. The past is gone and can't be changed; the future hasn't come yet. The only place we can do our work, spiritual or otherwise, is in the present.

Another way of looking at the past, present, and future is the approach to repentance taught by Hazreti Ali, the Fourth Caliph of Islam. He said there are three aspects to repentance—past, present, and future. Repentance of the past involves seeing clearly what we did that merits repentance. That means avoiding either self-blame or self-justification. Instead, we should look clearly and unjudgmentally at just what we did or didn't do. How can we change something if we don't understand it? Repentance of the present is to actively seek to correct whatever we did wrong. This may mean to apologize for what we said or to pay back what we took. Repentance of the future is to make it our intention not to repeat our past mistakes and to act on that intention. For example, if drinking is a problem, we would get rid of all the alcohol we have at home. Dwelling on the past without helping change

Divine Remembrance in the Sufi Tradition   165

anything is a waste of time. Fantasies or anxiety over the future are also useless and great time wasters. So that is why we are cautioned against these things.

In the Sufi tradition there is something called "remembering death." What does that mean?

As with almost every mystical tradition, remembering death helps reduce our attachment to the world. For some reason we forget death and think we're going to be here forever, so therefore the world gets really important. I'll never forget years ago a young woman came up to Sheikh Muzaffer, and she said very sweetly, "You know, when you're here it's so wonderful. You're here and I understand the importance of remembering God and the importance of prayer, and the world out there seems unreal. And this world of prayer and spiritual striving and spiritual truth seems so real. But when you leave, little by little the world becomes more and more real to me. What can I do?" I think that's the experience we've all had on retreats or with spiritual teachers or a spiritual community. And Sheikh Muzaffer laughed and said, "That's easy, that's an easy question." And then he quoted an old, classical Islamic story.

He said, It's very simple. Remember death. If you remember death you won't be so attached to the world. It's an old prescription: go to graves, go to hospitals, look at people in intensive care on their deathbeds, go to funerals and know that that coffin in front of you will eventually be your home. Then the world won't seem so real or so important.

It's really very simple. We usually remember death intellectually: "Oh, sire. I know I'm going to die." But when the doctor says, "You have cancer and I don't know how much time you have but your time is limited," then we begin to remember death. Of course, we lie when we say we remember death; we think about death but we don't really know it, we don't really remember it. Technically, as a psychologist, I would call that psychotic. Because psychosis means denial of reality. Our grandparents, our great-grandparents—they all went. The evidence is very clear—we're going. And we live in denial of it.

There's a story that your teacher Sheikh Muzaffer tells about a Sufi saint who is exiled to a Greek island with shackles on his arms and legs and who eventually dies. And Sheikh Muzaffer says, "Actually he did not die, he became. Only animals die; real human beings become. Saints don't die, they become."

We call something "death," which has all kinds of connotations about endings, but those Sufis who know say it's not an ending, it's a beginning. The beginning of another life.

CHAPTER TWELVE

THE REMEMBRANCE OF PAST LIVES FROM THE TIBETAN BUDDHIST PERSPECTIVE

A CONVERSATION WITH SOGYAL RINPOCHE

> The elephant is the wisest of all the
> animals, the only one who remembers his
> former lives; and he remains motionless
> for long periods of time, meditating
> thereon.
>
> Buddhist text

ON THE NIGHT WHEN THE BUDDHA ATTAINED ENLIGHTENMENT, he is said to have recollected his previous lives:

> I remembered many, many former existences I had passed
> through: one, two births, three, four, five . . . fifty, one hundred . . .
> a hundred thousand, in various world-periods. I knew everything
> about these various births: where they had taken place, what my
> name had been, which family I had been born into, and what I
> had done. I lived through again the good and bad fortune of
> each life and my death in each life, and came to life again and
> again. In this way I recalled innumerable previous existences
> with their exact characteristic features and circumstances. This
> knowledge I gained in the first watch of the night.

Throughout Western history we also find an acceptance of reincarnation in the speculations of Greek philosophers such as

Pythagoras and Empedocles; in the writings of early Christian church fathers such as Origen, who believed in the "preexistence of souls" (the theory of reincarnation was accepted by Christians until the Council of Trent, held in A.D. 1545); among the Druids, Orphics, and Cathars; as part of the hidden teachings of the Gnostics, Jewish Kabbalists, and certain Sufi mystics; and in the writings of many poets, novelists, and artists. "Some of us have in a prior existence been in love with an Antigone," Percy Bysshe Shelley once declared to a friend, "and that makes us find no full content in any mortal tie." Even the tough-minded Voltaire once stated: "After all, it is no more surprising to be born twice than it is to be born once." Hundreds of millions of today's Hindus, Buddhists, Jains, Druzes, and Alevis, as well as many African, North American Indian, and Pacific Island tribes, all embrace the idea of past lives. It is interesting that a Gallup poll taken in 1982 found that nearly one in four Americans believe in reincarnation, many asserting that although one may not be able to prove the reality of reincarnation, one also cannot prove its impossibility.

In a romantic rendition of the myth of the origin of the Tibetans as a race of people, legend has it that in prehistoric times Avalokiteshvara, the Bodhisattva of Compassion, was born as a monkey and mated with an abominable snowlady, Tara, the Bodhisattva of Enlightenment Activity, who gave birth to the first human beings, and that that divine monkey eventually became the source of the line of the Dalai Lamas. About this the Tibetologist Glenn H. Mullin comments in *The Fourteen Dalai Lamas*: "This Tibetan myth of humans descending from primates thus predates Darwin and his *The Origin of Species* by several thousand years. The fact that it survived the advent of Buddhism in Tibet speaks strongly for its popularity, for Buddhism in India had claimed that humans were descended solely from the gods (or perhaps from beings hailing from another planet). It is curious that the Tibetans accepted so much of Buddhist doctrine from India, and yet maintained their ancient (and more anthropologically friendly) legend of the primate connection."

The Tibetan Buddhist perspective offers an invaluable insight into the understanding of reincarnation. One of the most important Tibetan authorities on these teachings is Sogyal Rinpoche, author of the acclaimed bestseller *The Tibetan Book of Living and Dying*. Born in Kham in eastern Tibet, Sogyal Rinpoche was recognized as the incarnation of Lerab Lingpa Tertön Sogyal, a teacher to the thirteenth Dalai Lama, by Jamyang Khyentse Chökyi Lodrö, one of the most revered spiritual masters of the twentieth century. Sogyal Rinpoche attended Cambridge University and went on to study with many masters of all schools of Tibetan Buddhism. He has been traveling around the world and teaching for more than thirty years and is the founder and spiritual director of Rigpa, the name he has given to his work and to the vehicle he is developing to serve the Buddha's teaching in the West.

Sogyal Rinpoche spoke to me from Lerab Ling, Rigpa's main center, in the south of France.

In Buddhism the doctrine of reincarnation is considered to be a self-evident truth. Could you simply explain the idea of the continuity of mind upon which the notion of rebirth depends?

Before we can speak about the continuity of mind, I think, first, it's important to understand what is meant by the mind itself. The Buddhist teachings offer an extraordinary understanding of the mind and a complete methodology for working with and mastering our mind and its emotions. In fact, many people have called Buddhism "a science of mind."

What do the Buddhist teachings say essentially about the mind? *The mind is the root of everything.* In the Tibetan teachings, mind is called "the king who is responsible for everything"—*kun jé gyalpo*—the universal ordering principle. The mind is the creator of happiness and the creator of suffering, the creator of samsara and the creator of nirvana. Samsara is the cycle of existence, birth and death, characterized by suffering and determined by harmful emotions and our actions, or karma. Nirvana is, literally, the state beyond suffering and sorrow. One master put it: "Samsara is mind turned outwardly, lost in its projections. Nirvana is mind turned inwardly, recognizing its true nature."

And as the great guru Padmasambhava, who brought Buddhism to Tibet, said, "Don't seek to cut the root of phenomena. Cut the root of the mind." That's why I find these words of Buddha so inspiring: "We are what we think. All that we are arises with our thoughts. With our thoughts we make the world. Speak or act with an impure mind, and trouble will follow you, as the wheel follows the ox that draws the cart. We are what we think. All that we are arises with our thoughts. With our thoughts we make the world. Speak or act with a pure mind, and happiness will follow you, as your shadow, unshakable."

So changing our thoughts can change both ourselves and the world.

Yes. In fact, one of the mind's most marvelous qualities is that it can actually be transformed. The mind is like a crystal. It's so clear and so pure. Just as a crystal adopts the color of whatever surface you place it on, the mind will become just whatever we allow to occupy it. As Buddha said, "With our thoughts we make the world," and we are the makers of a world that we enjoy or we suffer in, a world of karmic phenomena fashioned by our thoughts and actions.

So we make this world of ours. And if we're able to change the one who makes it, naturally our world will change. Therefore, when you conquer your own mind, you also become master of your perceptions. When you're in control of your perceptions, you're automatically in control of states like fear and anxiety. And when you transform your perceptions, even appearances and experiences will begin to change. If only we were to remember this, keep it in our hearts and keep our heart and mind pure, then happiness would really follow. The whole of Buddha's teaching, then, is directed towards taming this mind and keeping our heart and mind pure.

I feel that nowadays, in the twenty-first century, what so many people are seeking is to find the truth of themselves and thereby the true nature of their minds. Everybody seems to be asking, "Who am I?" yearning to realize their true selves beyond the ego-self. So who are we, really? Are we our thoughts, our emotions, and our stories? Are all these things that we usually identify ourselves as really us? We seem to take our thoughts and emotions so seriously, give them so much importance, and hold on to them as solid and real. So much so that when we feel happy or have positive thoughts, we think that's who we are, or on the other hand, when we feel bad or have negative thoughts, that's who we think we are.

But if we really look, we see that everything we normally identify with as "ourselves" is actually always changing. Our thoughts are always changing, our emotions are always changing, our stories are always changing. We're not who we were yesterday or who we will be tomorrow. We're not who we were in childhood or who we will be in our old age. If we really look, all these thoughts, emotions, and stories are impermanent and constantly changing. They appear because of the interdependence of certain causes and conditions. These causes and conditions have their own particular time span, and when it's exhausted, then none of these thoughts, emotions, and stories remain. They appear because of the collision of a particular set of causes and conditions.

When we talk about things being connected interdependently, we're speaking about a process of change that involves many different causes and conditions. Yet so often in our lives, when things go wrong, we single out one particular cause, one person, one aspect of the situation as the object of our blame or anger. Now if we can only see that in fact what's happening has countless causes, all related to one another in a complex and intricate pattern, our whole attitude and way of thinking will expand. It will not make much sense to blame one person or one circumstance. As a result, the intensity of our emotions and reactions is weakened and undermined, and our anger and clinging are made groundless, as that single object that was their target has been removed. So interdependence serves a very practical and useful purpose in our daily life.

As I was saying, these causes and conditions themselves all

have their own individual life spans, and when they're exhausted, then none of these thoughts, emotions, and stories can endure. The same holds true in fact for anything that we normally think of as "us." Take your body, for example. Is it solid, permanent, and independent? If we examine it minutely, it breaks down into cells and molecules and even subatomic particles. Modern science even suggests that there is no such thing as "matter," only a field of energy and light.

What about our mind, then? Look at your mind and your thoughts. If you look for a past thought, you'll find you've missed it; it's already gone. If you look for a future thought, you can't find it because it has not yet arisen. Even the present moment, as soon as we start to think about it, has already passed. One of my masters, Dilgo Khyentse Rinpoche, used to say you can never have a thought in the present: "Past thoughts have vanished, there is nothing left of them. Future thoughts have not yet arisen at all. And in no way can present thoughts exist by themselves without depending on past and future thoughts." So when we really break it down, there's actually nothing that we can hold on to and say, "This is my mind."

So when everything is shifting and changing, is there anything about us that's constant or unchanging? In other words, what is the fundamental, true nature of our mind or our being? Who are we really? If we can understand this one thing, it can be such an extraordinary help. It can save us from enslavement to our thoughts and emotions. Because we will realize, when a thought arises, that it's not really us. What we are is so much more. The main cause of all our suffering is not knowing who we really are, so if we can really discover our real nature, and if we can make it into our reality, it is the source of freedom, happiness, contentment, and peace.

So what is our true nature?

Many times I have conversed with my Tibetan lama friends to see if there is a way in which we can understand, in a straightforward, down-to-earth way, what our true nature, the buddha nature, re-

ally is. One way to describe it is like this: From this morning
when we woke up, now while we are speaking, and tonight until
we go to bed, we will have lived with an awareness, a clear, knowing kind of consciousness. During the day, we will have many different thoughts and emotions. We may be happy, agitated, angry,
excited, sad, expectant, afraid, or bored, but while our moods and
feelings might change, this continuity of clear, vivid awareness is
always there, whatever we experience.

This clear awareness or cognizance—the knowing quality of
mind—dwells in our fundamental mind-stream. It is our mind at
its purest and most fundamental. This awareness is connected
not only with our mind but also with our heart. It's not only that
which knows but that which feels and understands. It's pure
feeling, pure heart. Even amidst the turmoil of our changing
thoughts, emotions, and fantasies, our fundamental consciousness, this pure awareness, this basic continuum or "mind-stream,"
is always with us, constant and unchanging. But we shouldn't
make the mistake of thinking of it as some kind of entity that exists as something solid, substantial, or independent. It's constant
and unchanging but not permanent.

This awareness has always been with us and will always be
with us throughout our lifetime. It was there when we were
young, and it will be there when we are old. It's there when we
are happy, and it's there when we're sad. It's there when things are
going well, and it's there when we're in trouble. It's there when
we are lonely. It's always there. It's said that this fundamental
pure consciousness, this pure awareness of ours, will continue
until enlightenment. And this is who, or what, we really are.

When you come to a deep understanding of this clear awareness, it can be called the buddha nature or the innermost, essential nature of mind. As the Dalai Lama says: "This consciousness
is the innermost subtle mind. We call it 'the buddha nature,' the
real source of all consciousness. The continuum of this mind lasts
even through buddhahood."

So when we say we have the "potential" for buddhahood or
enlightenment, it's in this fundamental pure consciousness.
However deeply you look into your mind, finally it's this that you

will end up finding. In the practice of meditation, if you can leave your mind unaltered and look deeply within, what you'll find is a pure awareness, a knowing quality of mind which understands and feels and which is the basis of everything.

How does this state of enlightenment relate to the idea of reincarnation?

Now this very subtlest level of consciousness, which we can call buddha nature, is what the Dalai Lama says "lasts even through buddhahood." Most people take the word *reincarnation* to imply there is some "thing" that reincarnates, that travels from life to life. But in Buddhism, we don't believe in an independent and unchanging entity like a soul or ego that survives the death of the body. What provides the continuity between lives isn't an entity, we believe, but this ultimately subtlest level of consciousness.

Some people argue that consciousness, or the ability to experience, depends on our physical body; they believe that consciousness exists in the brain, so that when the body dies, then consciousness dies as well, so that there can be no reincarnation. But according to the Buddhist scriptures, there are many levels of consciousness, some gross and some subtle. Some are dependent on the physical body and some aren't.

From the Buddhist point of view, the main argument that "establishes" rebirth is one based on the profound understanding of the continuity of consciousness, the subtlest level that is not dependent on the physical body. To try to explain this simply, we can ask: Where does consciousness come from? It can't rise from nowhere. A moment of consciousness can't be produced without the moment of consciousness that immediately preceded it.

His Holiness the Dalai Lama often explains it as follows: Everything is subject to change, or impermanence, and to causes and conditions, or interdependence. So there is no place given to a divine creator, nor to beings who are self-created; rather everything arises as a consequence of causes and conditions. So mind, or consciousness, *also* comes into being as a result of its previous causes and conditions.

Take physical matter as an example of this continuity of causes and conditions. Whatever it may be, it's said that it must possess what is called a "continuity of type" and a "continuity of substance." Let's take the example of a flower.

In the case of a flower, "continuity of type" simply means that the flower grows from the seed of an identical type of flower. On the other hand, "continuity of substance" means that the flower comes from a seed, that seed itself came from another flower, and so on backwards in a continuous succession that stretches back hundreds of millions of years.

We can say, in fact, that the *potential* for the existence of this flower—its "continuity of substance"—was present even when the earth first came into being, because even then the atomic particles existed that eventually, through a continuous process of evolution, would form the elements which make up our flower. So the continuity of substance is beginningless.

Just like the material world, consciousness must have a continuum in the past. If you trace our present mind or consciousness back, then you'll find that you're tracing the origin of the continuity of mind, just like the origin of the material universe, into an infinite dimension; it is, as you will see, beginningless. So there must be successive rebirths that allow that continuum of mind to be there.

When we talk of causes and conditions, there are two principal types: substantial causes, the stuff from which something is produced, and cooperative factors, which contribute towards that causation. In the case of mind and body, although one can affect the other, one cannot become the substance of the other—mind and matter, although dependent on one another, can't serve as substantial causes for each other.

So when someone is reborn, can we say that he or she is the same person that has died or a different person?

In the Buddhist scriptures, this is explained in a famous dialogue between a king named Milinda and the Buddhist sage Nagasena. The king asked Nagasena this same question: "When someone is reborn, is he the same as the one who just died, or is he different?" Nagasena replied: "He is neither the same nor different. . . . Tell me, if a man were to light a lamp, could it provide light the whole night long?" The king said, "Yes."

Nagasena asked, "Is the flame then which burns in the first watch of the night the same as the one that burns in the second . . . or the last?" The king said, "No." Nagasena asked again, "Does that mean there is one lamp in the first watch of the night, another in the second, and another in the third?" The king answered, "No, it's because of that one lamp that the light shines all night." Then Nagasena said, "Rebirth is much the same: one phenomenon arises and another stops, simultaneously. So the first act of consciousness in the new existence is neither the same as the last act of consciousness in the previous existence nor is it different."

I've always liked the example given by H. W. Schumann in his book *The Historical Buddha:* "The successive existences in a series of rebirths are not like the pearls in a pearl necklace, held together by a string, the 'soul' which passes through all the pearls; rather they are like dice piled one on top of the other. Each die is separate, but it supports the one above it, with which it is functionally connected. Between the dice there is no identity, but conditionality."

One of the things that occurred when the Buddha attained enlightenment was the recollection of his former lives. Is a heightened personal awareness a precondition for the remembrance of our past lives, and why can't we recall them?

On the night that Buddha attained enlightenment, in the very first stage of awakening, he vividly remembered all his past lives in great detail. However, knowledge about rebirth isn't exclusive to Buddhism. Since the dawn of history, reincarnation and a firm faith in life after death have occupied an essential place in nearly all the world's religions. Belief in rebirth existed among Christians in the early history of Christianity, and traces persisted down into the Middle Ages. Origen, one of the most influential of the church fathers, believed in the "preexistence of souls." He wrote in the third century: "Each soul comes to this world reinforced by the victories or enfeebled by the defeats of its previous lives." References to reincarnation can be found throughout history in some of the most unexpected places.

There are also many accounts of "ordinary people" from our own time who have memories of previous lifetimes. I often think of one particular story about a girl in the Punjab in India. Her memories of a past life came to the attention of the Dalai Lama, who sent his special representative to investigate and verify her account. One day the girl, whose name was Kamaljit Kour, suddenly asked her father to take her to another village, which was quite far away. Her father was taken aback and asked her why. Then it just streamed out of her. She told him: "I don't live here. This isn't my home. When I was riding home from school with a friend on my bicycle, we were hit by a bus. My friend died immediately. I was taken to the hospital, but they said I was bleeding so much I wouldn't survive, so I asked my parents to take me home to die." Kamaljit's father was stunned by the story, but she insisted, so finally he gave in and took her to the other village to pacify her.

As they arrived, she recognized the village from some distance and pointed to the place where she had been hit by the bus. Then they got into a rickshaw, and Kamaljit gave directions to the driver. The rickshaw stopped at a group of houses. Kamaljit got out and headed straight for the house where she said she had lived, but first her father, who did not believe her, asked the neighbors if there had been a family that lived nearby who lost their daughter. To his amazement, the neighbors said that Rishma, the daughter of the family in the house Kamaljit was heading for, had been hit by a bus and died at the age of sixteen on the way home from the hospital. Kamaljit ran to the house. Once inside, she greeted all of her former relatives by name and without mistake, then headed for her old room and asked for the things she'd owned. When it was time to catch the bus home with her father, Kamaljit refused to leave.

As the two families, Kamaljit's and Rishma's, started to put the pieces of the story together, they discovered that Rishma had died ten months before Kamaljit had been born. Even though Kamaljit had not started school yet, she would pretend to read. She could name all of her classmates in Rishma's school picture. And she would always ask for dark red clothes. Shortly before her death, Rishma was given a new dark red suit, which she loved but had never had the time to wear. The last thing that Kamaljit remembers of her past life was the headlights of the car going out on the way back from the hospital—this must have been when Rishma died. Interestingly enough, neither set of parents believed in reincarnation, but after they heard Kamaljit talk so vividly about her previous life, they had to change their minds.

This is just one extraordinary story. But most of us have no recollection of our past lives. Which is not surprising. We can barely remember what we were doing or thinking yesterday, or last Friday, let alone the specifics of our own childhood. When I think of my own childhood in Tibet, and then in exile in India and Sikkim, it seems as if I have lived so many lives just within this one lifetime. They all played their parts, but they are finished and over. They do not feel like "me." So if our memories of this life have almost totally eroded, it follows that it might not be easy or normal to remember what we were doing in a previous lifetime. Plato had an intriguing metaphor for this: he tells a story of what sounds like a near-death experience, where a soldier in an after-death state witnessed those who were about to be reborn. They were required to drink from "the River Unmindfulness," and as they did so they forgot absolutely everything.

But we don't have all the answers. We don't know how or why some people have memories of past lives. One possibility has been suggested by the Dalai Lama. It could be that the memory of past lives is dependent on the kind of death we have. When people die after a long illness or of old age, their memories of their lifetime are not vivid, and their consciousness and awareness aren't so strong. Whereas if people die young, when their faculties are very alert, and suddenly in violent circumstances, then because they're passing away in a very conscious, alert state of mind, perhaps there might be a stronger possibility of memories passing on into their next lives.

But does the fact that we simply cannot remember a previous life mean that we have never lived before? Wouldn't it be like saying Tibet doesn't exist just because we've never heard of it or been there? Don't we just limit ourselves with the conviction that rebirth doesn't exist? Doesn't it make more sense to give the possibility of a life after death the benefit of the doubt or at least be open to it? Aren't we merely limiting ourselves with our "conviction" that rebirth doesn't exist?

You mentioned earlier that, as Buddha awakened into the omniscient state of enlightenment, one of his realizations was the memory of former lives. It's interesting that one of the kinds of clairvoyance that comes with very advanced deep meditation practice is said to be knowledge of previous lives. As the mind is freed of its limitations, so the whole landscape of living and dying, the space in which our own lives and deaths take place, is progressively revealed.

What simply is the relationship between karma and reincarnation?

First of all, I'd like to say a few words to clarify a bit what is meant by *karma*, because we often misuse the word *karma* completely, throwing it around to mean fate or predestination. But the word *karma* is literally translated as "action." The Dalai Lama says: "Karma refers to intentional action." It's best understood as the infallible law of cause and effect that governs the universe. It's both the power latent within actions and the results our actions bring. To put it simply, this means that whatever we do, with our body, speech, or mind, will have a matching result. Each action, even the smallest, is pregnant with its consequences. The traditional Buddhist teachings explain at length the range of effects produced by our positive or negative actions specifically in terms of what kind of rebirth we have.

One thing determines the effect of our actions: our motivation, intention, and attitude. It's not the scale or size of our physical actions or words that counts but our motivation—our heart's deepest intention. As Buddha said: "We are what we think." The masters say even a little poison can be the cause of death, and even a tiny seed can grow into a huge tree. Buddha said: "Do not overlook negative actions merely because they are small; however small a spark may be, it can burn down a haystack as big as a mountain." Similarly he said: "Do not overlook tiny good actions, thinking they are of no benefit; even tiny drops of water in the end will fill a huge vessel."

So it's our motivation, good or bad, that determines the fruits of our actions. When we harm others, the one we are truly harming is ourselves. When we help others, ultimately it's ourselves that we are helping. This is why the Dalai Lama often used to say that if you really wish to be selfish, at least be "wisely selfish" rather than foolishly selfish. Take a good look, and you will realize that if you truly wish to take care of yourself, it means giving up harming others and trying to help them instead.

The masters always say that if you can't help, at least do not cause harm or harbor malice and hatred. If you think about interdependence, you come to realize what it means, even solely for your own happiness: that harming others harms you and helping others helps you. Reflect on this further and it will dawn on you that your happiness and your suffering are intimately connected with the happiness and suffering of others. All of us are linked. Not only are we affecting ourselves but because of interdependence we are affecting others, too. So we have to be responsible, not only for ourselves but for the world. And when we acknowledge our interdependence with one another, it naturally inspires us with a sense of *altruism* and spurs us towards helping others. As the great eighth-century Buddhist saint Shantideva says:

> Whatever happiness there is in this world
> All comes from desiring others to be happy.
> And whatever suffering there is in this world
> All comes from desiring oneself to be happy.

Karma does not decay, fade, or ever stop working. It cannot be destroyed. Its power will never disappear, until it's ripened. Although the results of our actions may not have matured yet, they will. Usually we forget what we do, and it's only long after the fact that the results catch up with us. But by then we're unable to connect them with their causes. So we usually assume that things just happen to us by chance. In fact, the results of our actions are often delayed, even into future lifetimes. And even then, we cannot pin down one cause because any event can be an extremely complicated mixture of many karmas ripening together.

As Buddha said, "What you are is what you have been, what you will be is what you do now." Padmasambhava went further: "If you want to know your past life, look into your present condition; if you want to know your future life, look at your present actions." The kind of birth we will have in the next life is determined by the nature of our actions in this one.

But again, karma is not predestination or fatalistic. Karma means our ability to create and to change. It is creative because we can determine how and why we act. We can change. Because everything's impermanent, as I mentioned earlier, things do not have a fixed existence and they're fluid, so whatever we do can provoke changes. And as everything is interdependent, whatever we do, whatever we say, and especially whatever we think has tremendous power. Otherwise, if nothing mattered, we might just as well say: "Eat, drink, and be merry, for tomorrow we die."

Everything does matter, because everything's interconnected with everything else. We matter. We are our own creators, as the creators of our karma and our own happiness and our own suffering. Our future is in our hands. There's no situation, however seemingly hopeless or terrible, which we cannot use to our benefit. And there's no crime or cruelty that sincere regret and real spiritual practice can't purify.

There is a saying, "Negativity has one good quality—it can be purified." (In Tibetan, this negativity is called *dikpa*, which is equivalent to the Christian word *sin*.) So there's always hope. Even murderers and the most hardened criminals can change and overcome the conditioning that led them to their crimes. Tibet's greatest yogin, poet, and saint, Milarepa, has an amazing life story. When he was young, Milarepa trained to be a sorcerer and out of revenge murdered and ruined countless people with his black magic. And yet through his remorse and the ordeals and hardships he went through with his master Marpa, he was able to purify all these negative actions and went on to become enlightened. Through his example, he became the inspiration for millions of spiritual practitioners everywhere.

It's interesting that many of those who undergo a near-death experience speak about a "life review," in which they relive or remember in great detail not only the experiences of their lives but also the effect that their thoughts, words, and actions have had on others. Some say that not a single thought or emotion is lost. And many say that when they're shown their lives in this way, they feel they're judging themselves. In the description of the after-death state in *The Tibetan Book of the Dead*, there's a judgment scene in which the dead person's good or bad actions are all totaled up. I find there's an intriguing parallel between this judgment scene and the life review. Because ultimately all judgment takes place within our own minds. We are the judges and the judged. The life review and the judgment scene also show that, in the final analysis, what really counts is the motivation behind our every action, and there is no escaping the effects of our past actions, words, thoughts, and the imprints and habits they have stamped us with. It means we're entirely responsible, not only for this life but for our future lives as well.

You've written that the belief in reincarnation demonstrates to us that there is some kind of ultimate justice or goodness in the universe. What did you mean by that? What effect does understanding something like karma have on a person's approach to life?

Whatever is happening to us now mirrors our past karma. If we really realize that, we'll also know that when suffering comes, it's never without a reason or a cause, that it's destructive emotions and negative actions, or karma, which stem from ignorance. Suffering does not just land on us from out of nowhere, it's the result of our past actions, the karma. However, if someone's suffering, it doesn't mean that he or she is somehow a "bad" person or that the suffering is a failure or a punishment in any way, but rather it means that person is finishing, purifying, or coming to an end of a particular karma. If we can recognize this and see our suffering as a purification, then suffering is given meaning and purpose.

Also, spiritual practice can quicken the process of purification, with the result that practitioners may not have to endure prolonged suffering over many aeons or lives. The suffering is done away with more quickly. This is how practitioners come to see suffering with joy, like a broom that sweeps away all our negative karma. Then not only do we see suffering for what it truly is but in the process we accumulate tremendous positive karma.

On the other hand, if we don't see suffering as a natural part of samsara—a fact of life—or as having a cause and a meaning, not only do we have to endure the suffering but we mishandle it as well. We will not use suffering well and draw out its true purpose. Instead, if we get anxious and alarmed and develop a strong aversion to suffering, this will not only block us from our path or spiritual development but also aggravate and magnify our suffering. This in turn might make us commit more harmful actions and create negative karma, which will result in even more and even worse suffering.

The same holds true for happiness. When happiness actually comes, we should try to recognize and appreciate what great good fortune it is to have happiness, and realize that it's the result of our previous good karma. When things are going well for us, then we should use it to strengthen ourselves and help others. Not waste it but instead invest it in positive wholesome actions, such as spiritual practice, which will bring about further and more happiness, leading to lasting happiness for both ourselves and others. If we don't invest happiness well, then we'll squander it and end up just where we started.

Karma can have a vivid and practical meaning in our everyday lives. You can see this with the Tibetan people—they live out the principle of karma, in the knowledge of its truth, and this is the basis of Buddhist ethics. They understand it to be a natural and just process. So karma inspires in them a sense of personal responsibility in whatever they do. But karma is something that all of us can actually see in action in our own lives. For example, think back to a time when you upset or hurt someone. Didn't it rebound on you? Weren't you left with a bad memory and shadows of self-hatred? That memory and those shadows are karma. Our habits and our fears too are due to karma, the results of actions, words, or thoughts we have done in the past. If we examine our actions and become really mindful of them, we'll see that there is a pattern that repeats itself in our actions. Whenever we act negatively, it leads to pain and suffering; whenever we act positively, it eventually results in happiness.

The most important point about believing in karma is the effect it has on how we live our lives—it will inspire us to lead a good life because we know that our actions, words, and thoughts will have an effect. The teachings tell us that for lifetimes we have been connected to one another, as brothers, sisters, husbands, wives, mothers, fathers, children, and enemies. We have been through everything together. As if we were all wrapped up in one another's lives, we have a relationship with others that is timeless and extraordinarily profound. In this vision the whole world becomes our closest family. So even if we aren't sure about reincarnation, just living our lives according to these principles can give life more meaning, a wider perspective, and a deeper vision.

PART THREE

AFTERTHOUGHTS

When you awake
You will remember everything.

Richard Manuel–Robbie Robertson,
"When You Awake"

YOU REALLY HAVE TO LOSE YOUR MEMORY TO REALIZE WHAT you've been missing.

There is a Mexican proverb: "You can't take from me what I've danced." But an erasure of memory takes exactly that—you cannot recall your last waltz. As Oliver Sacks writes: "Something has happened to someone's nervous system; and because of this, something has happened to someone's being." At a loss for memory, the result of what neurologists quaintly call "an insult to the brain" (in my case probably damage to the hippocampus and the temporal lobes), I don't really know or recognize that person I presume I used to be or his relation to the me I am now. I am not the person whose memories I do not recall—I am neither the person I was nor, strangely, the person I seem to be; and I often feel like an impostor to myself, being someone other than who I am. (Sometimes I wish I could go back to being the person I was, and sometimes not.) There is an almost total disconnect—an erasure of place and time like the erasing of a blackboard—with regard to what I was supposed to have done and experienced. In the *Confessions*, Saint Augustine writes of encountering himself in the halls of memory, saying, "I meet myself and recall what I am, what I have done, and when and where and how I was affected when I did it." From my own present vantage point, however, it often seems that I might as well not have lived my lost years, because *I was not there.* (Conversely, as they say about the 1960s, "If you *remember* them, you weren't there!") Cherished moments from the past are no longer registered.

In one of his sonnets, Shakespeare parsed my plight:

> Thy gift, thy tables are within my brain
> Full charactered with lasting memory,
> Which shall above that idle rank remain,
> Beyond all date, even to eternity:
> Or, at the least, so long as brain and heart
> Have faculty by nature to subsist;
> Till each to razed oblivion yield his part
> Of thee, thy record never can be missed.

My memories no longer subsisting, I depend on friends and acquaintances to fill in my past, relying, of course, on the accuracy of their memories, and trusting them not to mischievously invent or embroider the events they are recounting. (I wouldn't know the difference.) Whenever, for example, I ask them about how and where we first met, I listen to their stories with incredulity, amazement, shock, bewilderment, regret, and often with great amusement and acute embarrassment about the things that the *I* I am now who was the *me* I don't remember apparently did.

My memoryless world resembles that of Mr. and Mrs. Martin in Eugène Ionesco's play *The Bald Soprano,* who sitting facing each other in their friends Mr. and Mrs. Smith's suburban London home confront the possibility that they have met each other before—perhaps in Manchester, England, where they discover they both come from, perhaps in the train compartment where five weeks earlier they seem to have sat opposite each other on a journey to London, where they both seem to live on the same street and in the same flat and where they sleep together in the same room and in the same bed. "How bizarre, curious, strange, dear lady," remarks Mr. Martin, "it is perhaps there that we have met." "How curious it is and what a coincidence!" replies Mrs. Martin. "It is indeed possible that we have met there, and perhaps even last night. But I do not recall it, dear sir." And it remains for *me*, too, to imagine and accept what I can't recollect.

Take the example of my Swedish friend Nina, who displays the indomitable independence and fearlessness of Pippi Long-stocking and who is still incredulous that I am completely unable to recall anything about our first meeting, our times and travels together, our *histoire*. (Another friend has suggested that even if I do not remember persons I loved and knew during the years of my forgetfulness, I do have a continuing sense of their *essence* and added, "What else do you need to know?") Nina tells me that I met her during the summer of 1996, when I was living and writing in a small, traditional red-painted wooden cottage on the coast of southwestern Sweden. (Difficult as it is to believe, I have no recollection of having lived in that cottage for four summers; I have only a dim memory of that one summer of 1996.) Of this cottage I can remember in a vivid, lightning-illuminating flashback its driveway, the small bedroom with a gray rotary phone on a desk extending out from a wall, and outside—this recollection with the help of a photograph—in the back of the cottage, under several ash trees, a wooden deck (with a wooden table and four blue-cushioned chairs), beneath which were numerous ensor-celled rocks (so magical they seemed to me that I carried a beautiful black one back to the United States) that jutted down to the Kattegat Sea. It was a fairy-tale dwelling in the enchanted community of Kattvik, consisting of no more than three hundred hill- and seaside houses about four miles from the town of Båstad, which is the tennis mecca of Sweden.

In the fall of 2003, when I was visiting Sweden, in part, nostalgically, to revisit the Kattvik cottage, Nina asked me one afternoon in Malmö, where she now lives, whether I didn't want to hear her account of how we first met in Kattvik in order to give me an idea of some of the delightful things I'd forgotten, and suggested that I include it in my memory book as a testament and in order to bear witness to a vanished and idyllic time.

So how did we meet?

How did we meet. The first time. The first time I was driving . . .
do you remember my friend Ulrika? She, her boyfriend, and I
were going to Wivika and Philippe's wedding, which you were
going to as well and which was taking place just outside of
Kattvik, where you were staying that August. So I was driving my
friends up from Lund, where I was living at the time. And it was
a very hot day, so we somehow stopped in Kattvik at your cottage.
And I wanted to take a swim because it was so warm and it was a
beautiful, beautiful place, this Kattvik place. And your cottage
was right on the water, and I met you there and you said hello to
me there, and Ulrika, her boyfriend, and I went into the water to
take a swim, naked; there was nobody around who might get
upset. And I like that.

Then a few days later Calle, who you knew from Kattvik and
who was the boyfriend of someone I knew just a little, called me
and asked if he, you, and I could take a beer, just the three of us
together—you had obviously said something to him about wanting to see me again. And I said, Well, okay. So I went down from
my parents' house—they have a house up above Kattvik and I was
staying with them for a week—and bicycled to Båstad. And there
were you and Calle, and we went to this little bar and you started
making these compliments to me . . . like, I don't know, about
everything, about how I had played the violin as a child and that
you had played the violin and that was extraordinary and that I
knew French linguistics and Spanish and German and Latin so
well—I was taking a course in Latin that summer—and that was
extraordinary and, I don't know, you had a lot of compliments.

And so we had a good time. And when I came home from that
encounter I thought: This guy is crazy if he thinks he's going to
have a date with me by being very, very sweet and complimen-
tary! And then a few days later you called up and said, Hello, this
is J. Cott [laughing]. And you started chitchatting and asked me
what my plans were for the week. I said I had to go to Lund because of the Latin course I was taking there. And I had a transport
problem because I didn't have a car and my mother's car was oc-

cupied and the train was really a hassle because it took so long
and you had to bicycle down to the railway station and then take
the train for one and a half hours and then walk from the railway
station . . . I mean, it would have taken me three hours to get from
point A to point B. So I sort of let this be, what do you say, *noted*.
And you said, Well, I can drive you there.

That was nice of me.

That was very nice. So you picked me up at my parents' place,
and I did the driving since I knew where we were going, and you
were a very amusing person. And I also had a Latin book with me,
so you rehearsed my homework with me. . . . You had some Latin,
didn't you?

Amo. Amas. Amat.

I love. You love. He loves.

Carpe diem [Seize the day].

Carpe diem. Anyway, there was this little drawing in the book
showing a pedagogue and two of his twelve-year-old disciples in a
room in ancient Greece. No, this is Latin, it had to be Rome.
Rome, no? No, this was Greece because he was a pedagogue.
And in the drawing one of the boys was standing up putting on
some clothes and the other one was sitting on his own bed, and
the pedagogue was holding some kind of jar and it looked like the
kid was spitting in the jar, and I guess you could misinterpret that
picture. I thought he was a pedagogue, and you told me you
thought he was a . . .

Pederast . . .

Anyway, we were talking and drove past the exit to Lund and
found ourselves on the way to Malmö, so I said we had to
make . . . what do you say, *faire le tour . . .*

A turn.

We had to turn around and go back to Lund, where I went to my course. Actually, before I went to my course you managed to buy me and my friend Ulrika two pairs of long johns, very nice long johns, red and white striped. And you bought other long johns for your ex-wife's daughter and some other children. You bought a lot of long johns that day [laughing]. So I went to my course, and afterwards you asked me if I wanted to have dinner with you. And I thought: Can I have dinner with this person without promising him anything? And you said, If we have dinner you don't have to do *anything* [laughing]. So I said, Okay, let's have dinner. So we had dinner in Lund at a restaurant called Petri Pumpa—Peter's Pumpkin—and we had a nice conversation. We weren't talking about stupid things but not about heavy, heavy things either. We had a really good time. And then we drove back, and I got out of the car at my parents' place and I slammed the door, and immediately after slamming the door, I said to myself, I *miss* this person. And you drove down to Kattvik. I don't know how the other encounters were put together, probably you called me, probably I was too terrified to do anything.

I'm almost too afraid to ask what happened then.

Then after seeing each other a few times, we went to Lund together and you came to my apartment, which I was sharing with my friend Signe. And that's when you asked me if I knew what a "snuggle" was [great laughter]. I was lying on my mattress on the floor, and you lay down next to me and said, "Do you know what a snuggle is?" And I said, "No, what is a snuggle?" and then you showed me!

You don't even have an image of this?

Not at all.

What a pity!

•   •   •

It's a pity to forget the past. It's also a pity to forget how to live in the present. Often I feel alone in my forgotten and forgetting world, and search for those who have trodden the same path as I have. Then one day a friend presented me with a book that perfectly, and perhaps one might say miraculously, mirrored my life. Opening the book, I read the first paragraph: "I used to be able to think. My brain's circuits were all connected and I had spark, a quickness of mind that let me function well in the world. I could reason and total up numbers, I could find the right word, could hold a thought in mind, match faces with names, converse coherently in crowded hallways, learn new tasks. I had a memory and an intuition that I could trust." *In the Shadow of Memory* by Floyd Skloot—a remarkable novelist, poet, and essayist—describes how a virus that he contracted in an airplane caused brain lesions that altered both himself and his life, lesions that, he writes, "disrupted the network that operates my short-term memory and swamped much of my long-term memory."

Unlike my own, his brain damage also manifested itself in disrupting specific motor functions such that he had problems tying his shoes or taking a shower or attending a party and had to use a cane. (After fourteen years he is now able to walk without it.) Unfortunately, like me, he suffers from the following symptoms of brain damage: a quantifiable diminishment in both IQ level and cognitive capabilities; a diminished ability to express himself; a need to be given instructions in small doses rather than all at once; the habit of endlessly repeating himself; an inability to recall things he has just thought; difficulty in watching a film and remembering dialogue after a few seconds; and the need to highlight nearly the entire text of a book in yellow and then, after picking up the book again, finding that he has little recall of what he has highlighted. Out of the blue I had discovered *mon semblable, mon frère* (my double, my brother) as Charles Baudelaire wrote.

I was able to make contact with Floyd Skloot, who lives in rural Oregon with his wife, Beverly, and he agreed to talk to me about his fractured life and about, as he writes, "how to live, how to be, especially when you find yourself at the end of your ability to know." He also spoke of the hard-won and ingenious ways, which I myself hope to try to imitate, that he has worked out to enable him to continue his life as an extraordinary writer whose essays—a number of which appear in *In the Shadow of Memory*—have been published in anthologies such as *The Best American Essays*, *The Art of the Essay 1999*, and *The Best American Science Writing 2000*. Floyd Skloot spoke to me on the phone from his home in Oregon.

Could you say something about what happened to you on December 7, 1998?

On that date I was flying from Portland, Oregon, where I was then living, in order to attend a conference in Washington, D.C. And it was on the plane that I believe I contracted the virus that targeted my brain. I was working as a senior public policy analyst for an electric power company, and the conference was about public power policy. At that time in my life I was forty-one and was in remarkable health and physical shape, and I'd been running and winning ribbons in long-distance races for years. In all, I felt and was in perfect condition.

And you were also thinking clearly?

Absolutely. My job required that I advise lobbyists who worked for the company in seven different states, and I was often on simultaneous phone calls with very complex issues to sort through quickly and provide immediate advice as to how the lobbyists should respond, and I was also doing research and writing papers for the company. I was working at a very high level, I think, of intellectual functioning. And I had published poetry quite widely, in *Harper's* and other magazines, and had finished the manuscripts of two novels that were published after I got sick. So yes, I was writing and receiving awards for my writing for years. And I was also raising a daughter and stepson, and had a very active life within the community.

What happened to you after you got off the plane in Washington?

The next morning I woke up and it was immediately clear that something was wrong. I thought I had the flu, a very serious flu. It immediately manifested itself with neurological symptoms. I woke up at six o'clock and couldn't really figure out what time it was. I couldn't process the difference in time between Washington and Portland, I couldn't figure out how to turn off my clock's alarm. You know, runners keep keys on their wrists when they go out to run. And when staying at the hotel I couldn't figure out how to insert the key onto the band. And I couldn't get on the elevator properly; I tried to get on before the door opened. Then I couldn't make sense of what was happening at the conference; I didn't understand the information I was being given. And it really took six to eight weeks after that that I came to a full stop.

I returned to Portland and continued trying to run, getting slower and slower and getting lost on a trail that I had run on every day for years. And at work I was beginning to be unable to function. I was unable to understand the information I was getting, I couldn't handle phone conversations, I couldn't complete a memo. Things that I needed to do, I simply forgot to do or did them wrong. I was even unable to find my way back from the coffee shop. I began noticing my malfunctions with regard to thought and reasoning and memory and concentration, the whole package. I was noticing all of this over the next six weeks. It didn't make sense, and I didn't know what was happening to me. I knew I had a problem, but it never came together until I couldn't run, couldn't work, couldn't do anything anymore and I came to a stop. It was devastating. And I didn't rest or seek medical help, I just tried to forge onward, and weakened and tired myself further. Then in January of 1989, I couldn't go to work, and I began looking for a diagnosis, so I went to a series of doctors. And it occurs to me, looking back, how fortunate I was that I was living in Portland and could access Oregon Health & Science University, where there were some marvelous practitioners who took me seriously even though my symptoms were bizarre and didn't add up to anything recognizable.

Did you see a neurologist there?

The doctor who really diagnosed and saved me was an internal medical practitioner—an infectious diseases specialist the bulk of whose practice was HIV patients. And he said almost immediately that I was suffering from some type of viral illness and that the dementia I was beginning to show was as grave as an AIDS dementia which he saw all the time. And through him I got to a neurologist and a neuropsychologist, and they were at least able to determine that I was suffering from some sort of postviral encephalopathy. And we proceeded from there with MRIs and various other scans to pinpoint the nature of the damage, which I describe in my book as punctate lesions—a scattershot of holes all over the brain's gray area.

So your brain cells were destroyed.

That's right. There was cell death and damage to the neurotransmitters and the neurochemistry.

Do you have any idea of how this virus was transmitted?

I think airplanes can be illness chambers in the sense that they recirculate the bad air—think of the cases of SARS transmitted on airplanes—and I suspect that a number of people were exposed to whatever virus this was, but my immune system was compromised during that period because of the intensive training I was doing for long-distance running. And there were a number of other stresses in my life at the time.

In In the Shadow of Memory *you talk about your problems when writing with pen and paper, saying your letters were jumbled, your words were missing, your sentences were colliding, and your spelling was contorted. The way you wrote really sounds like a mirror of your brain.*

That's exactly correct. When my wife, Beverly, and I were visiting Achill Island, off Ireland's northwest coast, I was forced to write using pen and paper rather than the computer—I was trying to compose by hand for the first time since my illness—and I looked at what I was writing and the page was indecipherable. And that problem is now completely disguised when I write on the computer: I type out what I can type out, fill in the blanks, I don't see the cross-outs or the fractured handwriting and spelling, and I'm able to correct everything before anyone sees the mistakes. One of the solutions for me has been working with the computer and working very slowly; the mess of it isn't thrust right into my face every time I compose.

But In the Shadow of Memory *is a beautifully written book: your writing displays a sense of nuance, flexibility, precision, stylistic gracefulness, and an astonishing command of language such that you can write wonderfully, for example, about your thoughts "teetering and toppling into fissures of cognition."*

A number of people have said that the evidence of the book itself seems to contradict what the book is saying. But I've been a poet all my life, and I'm not stupid, I'm just inefficient. I haven't lost language, I have easy access to it, and I've just learned to compose slowly over time and eventually get down on the page what I'm trying to say. An essay included in my book, "A Measure of Acceptance," took me eleven months to write. It looks polished, but that's the result of eleven months' composition, with long breaks when I couldn't work, then coming back and using whatever talent I may have to fill in the holes and see where I am going. So my book represents eight to nine years' worth of work, so that it now looks all coherent.

I find that when I speak I can't find the words I'm searching for and have to compensate for that by using other, less precise and intentional words. Do you have that problem?

Of course. It's because of our aphasia and paraphasia. There are a lot of simply idiotic things that I'm often saying because I'm using the wrong words. But I've also found that it's led me into some really nice discoveries. For example, I found myself describing my experience as being *geezered* overnight. I had confused the words *seizure* and *geezer*, and it just popped in.

I wish I could formulate such neologisms! I don't know if you have the same problem as I do, but I find it extremely difficult to remember a sentence or a paragraph in a text that I've just read.

Certainly. That's why the books I read are so covered in yellow highlights; it's a futile attempt to embed what I've just read into my head. I read it and read it again as I highlight it, thinking I can go back and find it again. But then the whole book is lost again when I return to it.

So how do you do all of your impressive research in the neuroscientific literature that you present in your book?

I read over and over and take notes—my note-taking really helps—and try to find ways to organize the materials so that I can find them again by keeping my notes together. So if I'm writing about certain kinds of neurological concepts, then I know where to find what I've previously read. And I sometimes speak certain sentences aloud during the reading of the book. Or stop and talk about it with Beverly. Those sorts of things surround what I've read with additional meaning, and they help to embed and encode that memory by stopping, repeating, talking about it, perhaps recognizing what I'm doing at the time that I read. All of these become clues that help me recall things when I need them.

When people hear someone complaining about severe memory problems, they usually say things like "You're just getting older," "Well, my memory is bad too," or "Join the club." Don't you find that most people can't really comprehend, imagine, or enter into the experience of what it's like to suffer from severe short-term and long-term memory loss?

Yes. And they don't see you moment to moment, when you struggle to piece these things together and to remember and to communicate. They see you perhaps at your best, they see you when you're willing to see them, and it looks a lot easier than it really is. And it's *not* the same as not remembering where you put your car keys or forgetting the name of the person who's coming across the room whom you met an hour ago. It's more than that, it's not an occasional event.

In your book you write that when people say things to you like "Well, I'm forgetting things all the time," you reply to them: "Yeah, well, can you learn how to use a new camera or boom box? Can you compute change from a ten-dollar purchase? Do you lose the fifty dollars you had in your pocket while you're browsing through a bookstore? Do you forget phone numbers in the act of dialing them? Do you get lost in your own neighborhood?"

You know, I don't say those things, those are the things I *wish* to say. I've found that the frustration and difficulties that arise when I'm interacting with people make it not worth doing. So I seldom go out, I'm seldom in those situations, I'm seldom with people whom I don't know and who don't know me and my story. And it's one of the ways that I sort of protect myself.

You write: "The damage done to a brain seems to evoke disdain in those who observe it and shame or disgrace in those who experience it."

That's right. As a child, I was the family's memory bank and was called upon to remember all sorts of things. In fact, I had a head for trivia, and I was overestimated because I had a good memory, but that didn't necessarily mean that I knew anything. It's a very ironic way to say that that is what a man is worth.

You also write that "becoming ill afforded me the chance to dis-cover my emotional state and align it with my new biological state." And you say that you are now "dwelling more in the wider realm of sense and emotion, out of mind and into body, into heart. An altered state."

I don't think it was easy to come to that state by any stretch. But I had the tremendous support from my wife, with whom I can talk through these things—she and I got married after I got sick, which is another amazing thing for a person in my condition, for you'd think that those days would be over when you might find and attract someone who could love you. You're not much in the world, you're not active, you can't dance, you're not great com-pany, you're not the kind of person to be of interest to somebody. I'm not exactly Brad Pitt. So I've been extremely fortunate, be-cause Beverly's support of me has really helped me to come back to where I am and to accept things.

In your book you frequently talk about being altered, about the world being off-kilter, and about feeling lost. "Even inside my head," you write, "there is a feeling of being lost, thoughts that go nowhere, emptiness where I expect to find words or ideas, dreams I never remember." It's haunting.

Yes. In your situation, don't you also find these things true?

I do.

It *is* haunting, and I think it requires some genuine coming-to-terms-with, if you can. You can't pretend that you're the way you were.

Sometimes I feel that to be in this state is actually amazing.

Yes, you didn't know it was possible to be like this.

*Speaking of feeling lost, the Spanish philosopher Ortega y Gasset
once wrote: "The man with the clear head is the man who frees himself from those fantastic 'ideas' and looks life in the face, realizes
that everything in it is problematic and feels himself lost. And this
is the simple truth—that to live is to feel oneself lost, and he who
accepts it has already begun to find himself to be on firm ground."*

I like that a lot, and it's true. Some of the way I deal with that lostness is just to recognize what I'm capable of and what I'm not capable of. To remember something I've forgotten. Or to put
together the poultry shears—the scissors come in two separate
pieces, and for the life of me I can't take them out of the drawer
and put them together. It's like a jigsaw puzzle that I can't do.
And if I'm up against something like that or something that I
need to accomplish or master, the harder I try, the more of a mess
I get into, the more confusing the whole labyrinth becomes. I've
had to learn how to try to master something, to step back, slow
down, try something else, somehow to overcome my lostness and
live in harmony with my limitations. And with the world. There
are just too many stimuli, and I can't focus on them. When I'm
giving a reading in a public forum and people ask questions, I'll
answer them, and people will say, Gee, you're just doing so well.
And I'll point out that I have no recollection of any of the questions that were asked of me before the question that had just been
asked and that I can't tell you who asked the question or spoke to
me, that I'm doing it in the moment. So memories are slipping
away as I'm in the middle of performing. And it took me years to
get to where I could even go out and do the performance.

Are you forgetting the questions I've just been asking you?

I have no recollection of what you've just asked me. None. I know
you called me a few minutes before two o'clock my time, but I
have no sense really of how long our conversation has gone on or
what you've asked me. Except for the last question, which was
whether I could remember the questions you've asked me. I'm

too busy answering you to do my encoding. I started taking notes at the beginning of our conversation so that I can tell Beverly what you were asking me, and I realized that I couldn't answer your questions if I did that, so I left the room I was in when we first spoke and now I'm lying on my bed talking to you so that there are no distractions.

There's tremendous benefit in discussing all of this with you. There's someone here who's going through what you're going through, and in some way that makes it less isolating.

THE WORLD IS FILLED WITH LOVE STORIES, BUT FEW OF THEM ARE as profoundly filled with as many facets of the world as the story of Isis and Osiris. These two Egyptian gods were both brother and sister, husband and wife. Their mother was Nut, Goddess of the Sky; their father was Geb, God of the Earth; and it is said that the twin brother and sister were already in love with each other in the womb of their mother.

As king and queen of Egypt in the first age of the world, Isis and Osiris bestowed on humankind the gifts of civilization. Osiris taught his subjects how to cultivate wheat, barley, and corn; introduced writing and astronomy; and trained the people to worship the gods. Isis provided medicines of healing and magical incantations, invented the loom, and dispensed the justice of the heart. Compassionate teachers of humanity, Isis and Osiris were at the moment of their conception a couple whose love transcended understanding.

But Osiris's loutish, cantankerous brother Set (who, along with his sister Nephthys, was also the offspring of Nut and Geb) was envious of his more famous and beloved sibling. One fateful, dark night, Osiris mistook Nephthys for Isis; the child of that illicit union was the jackal-headed god Anubis, guide of the souls of the dead in the underworld. Set harbored feelings of revenge.

And it came to pass that one night when the moon was full, Set and his entourage, out hunting, pursued a wild boar into the delta swamps and came upon the dead body of Osiris. In a rage,

Set cut his brother's body into fourteen pieces, one for each night of the waning moon, and then scattered them throughout the land of Egypt. Accompanied by her sister Nephthys, the grieving Isis traveled the whole of the country, from the Delta to Nubia, re-membering Osiris, as they remembered him in their hearts, for to remember is to heal. Isis and Nephthys re-collected each member of their brother's body—head, heart, backbone . . . all except the phallus, which had been swallowed by a fish in the Nile—and they proceeded to reassemble the god.

REMEMBERING IS HEALING. SINCE THE MID-1990S IN UGANDA, Kenya, and several other African countries, health workers have been encouraging patients dying of AIDS to preserve their memories in "memory books" for their soon-to-be-orphaned children. (There are more than 11 million AIDS orphans in Africa today.) Part photo album, part diary, these memory books are ordinary binders with plastic pages recounting and preserving the family history in written messages and diary entries (along with the parents' favorite Bible verses), recalling where a child was born, when he took his first steps, what his first day of school was like, as well as in photographs—grandparents in their tribal village, a mother with her daughter in her arms, a child on a bicycle—as well as, occasionally, a pressed butterfly or even grains of sand, emblematizing the lives soon to be lost.

Speaking about the special uses of photographs in African villages, Judith Gleason recalls seeing

> wonderful village photographers who throw a black cloth over their heads and take pictures of weddings, christenings, and baptisms. (When the church came in, it made a lot of conversions, and baptisms became one of the most significant features of village life.) And to some extent photographs have had to replace the oral tradition, especially since the very people who would have told the stories of the ancestors have died of AIDS. And as the society disintegrates, then whatever memories the living still have of the places where their families and their clan used to live

would be very important to set down. In Africa, religion depends
so much on locales—it's not as extreme as the songlines in Aus-
tralia, but the migration pattern of the family is very important.
And of course the children need to have this material, and the
memory books fill this need. And maybe some day the grandchildren will be able to visit their families' villages. Who knows?

Discussing these memory books in *The New York Times* of
April 2, 2003, Marc Lacey writes about Rebecca Nakabazzi, a
thirty-year-old Ugandan hairdresser and seamstress suffering from
AIDS. (As of 2004, 1.7 million children in Uganda had been or-
phaned by AIDS—a tenth of the world's total.) Frail and feverish,
she has created a memory book for her eleven-year-old son,
Julius, in which she offers advice that she wants him to follow and
tells of her own childhood and that of his father, who died when
Julius was two, also of AIDS. "You resemble your father and at the
same time me," she writes to Julius, "so you are a mirror of both
of us." And on a page devoted to things she loves about him she
says, "You are supportive. You would ask, 'Are you sick? You're not
feeling well? Sorry.' "

Putting together memory books is an often laborious and emotionally deracinating task. But parents who have completed them
report that the process can be joyful and inspiring as they recall
long-forgotten, treasured memories. And the books are healing for
the children as well: "Losing one's parents is always traumatic,"
writes Marc Lacey, "but advocates of the books say they can help
reduce the emotional void orphans face in the future even if their
own futures are also cut short by the virus, as is often the case. Julius
himself has been diagnosed with the virus that causes AIDS."

Shortly before her death, Rebecca Nakabazzi said, "When we
die a lot of memories can fade away with us. The family history
can disappear. I want Julius to always remember his mother."

HOW DO YOU COLLECT AND RE-COLLECT MEMORIES THAT ARE NO
longer there? In *Spiritual Dimensions of Psychology*, Hazrat Inayat Khan offers up the following possibility: "A person who has

lost his memory owing to a disorder," he writes, "still has a memory just the same, and that memory will become clearer to him after death." (It's always said that, at the moment of death, the memories of one's entire life flash before one's eyes.) But in this life, friends are a redeeming solace, reminding you about who and what you were when you had forgotten, encouraging you to sense the joy of imagining a world of lost emotions, and priming you for a future in which obstacles can, as Jorge Luis Borges once said about his blindness, become a "resource."

As a friend once told me: "If you can't write the way that you used to, there's some other way to connect to an ecstatic simplicity that doesn't need memory for its expression." A Spanish psychologist asked one of my friends to remind me that "in order to see the light, one doesn't need one's memory." And another friend suggested that I think of my lost memories as if they were like the millions of grains of colored sand in a Tibetan mandala sand painting, a cosmogram representing both sacred consciousness and a sacred model of the world—grains later to be dispersed according to Buddhist practice, suggesting the impermanence of life. Like memories drifting away.

Some of the strangest words of comfort I received came from my friend Hanna Wolski—a student of the esoteric tradition— words that sent me spinning: "During electroshock," she informed me,

> what happens is that your etheric body gets completely shattered and it destroys the fibers and connections between your physical and etheric bodies and creates huge blockages of the natural flow of energy because the *prana*—the life-sustaining energy given to us by the sun—is received and distributed through our etheric body. Called *Ka* by the Egyptians or *pranayama kosha* by the Vedantics, this vital envelope of the physical body is part of a multidimensional torus tube-shaped electromagnetic field surrounding our physical body. Damage of the etheric body has to be repaired by a very evolved or advanced healer or ascendant master, a multidimensional healer and higher being who can sew your body together.

But regardless of having any problems with memory-related diseases like Alzheimer's or with memory loss from aging or from your shock treatments, there's the question of how one defines memory itself. I think memory is a certain continuum of moments that we can perceive in time in our mind, a certain continuum that we can recapitulate, going back and forth. There is, for instance, eidetic memory, which children have before the age of seven and which is very similar to Aboriginal memory and is closely linked to the work of the right hemisphere of our brain, although in the case of the Aboriginals, it goes further back to transpersonal and holographic memory . . . but that's another story.

Memory is in every single cell of our body. Memory is connected to your DNA—you can have memory of your ancestors, of your lineage. Memory is in a tree, in a bird, in a mineral, in a crystal, and in the sun. The Aboriginals, Native Americans, and other Earth Keepers pray to the sun, knowing well that it holds memories and keys to the reawakened encodings of their souls and of their divine purpose. Earth has a memory. Just as memory is held primarily by magnetic fields around our brain, inside the skull, and around our head, and then by magnetic fields around ourselves and, further, by the living electromagnetic fields around our body, so the earth has the magnetic grid which holds memories and levels of our awareness. And our ability to tap into this is relative to the state of our consciousness. The only question is how to access the continuum, and there are some ways of accessing it. It begins by searching for who you really are and what you are doing here. Through our constant verification, which leads to identification with the true self, through meditation and purification of our chakras, which sit in our etheric body and are true lenses by which we perceive reality, we allow an intelligible force—Divine Mother Kundalini Shakti—to work through us.

The electromagnetic shield around the earth was created for us in order that we lose memory. We are imprisoned in this frequency field, therefore only through practice of meditation and shifting into the sacred chamber of the heart can we raise our frequency to a certain vibrational rate that brings us back to constant memory. This process is called an ascension. Constant memory is what we call immortality, and it's a level of a higher state of awareness. Knowing that we are and always have been part of the Whole and Divine, this process of rejoining and returning to the Whole is called Remembrance. An ancient Rig-Veda prayer goes: "From darkness lead me to light. From unreal lead me to the real. From death lead me to immortality." It is called an evolutionary process, an ascent of personality and matter into spirit. Interestingly enough, there are traces of this Truth in other languages: *anamnesis* (to remember your true Self) and *smirti* (memory of one's divinity). The reverse process of evolution, where we endure self-amnesia, duality, and density through the lowering of our frequencies, is called "involution"—a process where the soul descends into matter and loses its memory.

Hanna's words have somehow persisted in my mind. But I am in the habit of taking the materialist view that if one's brain cells die—as they do because of Alzheimer's disease and probably, in the view of a number of neuroscientists, after electroshock treatments—one's personal memories no longer exist. The English biochemist Rupert Sheldrake, however, provocatively and encouragingly suggests otherwise. On a 1983 BBC radio program entitled *Living Memories*, he commented:

> Most people assume that memories are stored inside the brain, and the usual evidence for that is that damage to the brain can result in loss of memory. This doesn't actually prove anything one way or the other. If you cut out a bit of the circuitry of a TV set—remove the wires and transistors—the pictures on the screen will disappear. Now, that doesn't prove that all the people you see on the screen and the events that are going on there are stored inside the bits you've cut out. It merely proves that you're no longer able to tune in to them. Similarly, if you cut out a bit of the brain and lose the ability to have certain memories, it

doesn't prove that those memories are stored there. It merely shows that what you've cut out is necessary in some way for recovering or retrieving or tuning in to those memories.

Perhaps someday I will discover a way to tune in to my memories again. When I awake I will remember everything.

TO FORGET IS HUMAN, BUT FOR SOME, TO FORGET IS DIVINE. IT IS obviously not always beneficial to have intense, long-lasting memories, especially those that induce the kind of debilitating emotional arousal that can lead to post-traumatic stress disorder. There are, furthermore, some individuals whose astonishingly powerful memories result in unsuccessful lives. (Think of the case of S., as recounted in A. R. Luria's *Mind of a Mnemonist*.)

If Memory is the mother of the Muses, Forgetting, according to the eighteenth-century French writer Joseph Joubert, is their father. What is the lure of a forgetting mind? Sometimes it can protect you and even save your life. In Buchenwald, wrote the blind French Resistance leader Jacques Lusseyran in *And There Was Light*, "the feeble-minded, the ones who were short on memory and imagination . . . did not suffer. They lived from minute to minute, each day for itself, I suppose as beggars do. The odd thing was that it was comforting to be with them. The tramps, the hoboes, the ones who had never had a place to live, stupid and lazy as they were, had gathered up all kinds of secrets about living. They did not complain. They passed their secrets along. With them I spent many hours." In Yann Martel's novel *Life of Pi*, the protagonist, lost at sea, survives because he makes a point of forgetting, saying: "My story started on a calendar day—July 2, 1977—and ended on a calendar day—February 14, 1978—but in between there was no calendar. I did not count the days or the weeks or months. Time is an illusion that only makes us pant. I survived because I forgot even the very notion of time."

The great Russian poet Marina Tsvetaeva—herself one of the Muses—wrote: "A kiss on the head—wipes away memory. / I kiss your head" (translation by Elaine Feinstein). There are times

when all of us desire to be kissed on our heads in order to be be-
calmed of unhappy and unwanted remembrances of things past.
By contrast, Hazrat Inayat Khan believes that we can and must attain this state on our own. "How can one destroy undesirable
thoughts [and memories]?" he asks. "Must they always be destroyed by the one who has created them? Yes, it is the creator of
the thought who must destroy it; and it is not in every person's
power to do so. Yet the mind which has reached mastery, which
can create as it wishes, can also destroy. When we are able to produce on the canvas of our heart all that we wish and to erase all
we wish, then we arrive at that mastery for which our soul craves;
we fulfill that purpose for which we are here. Then we become
masters of our destiny."

In the sixteenth century the essayist Michel de Montaigne,
who confessed to being "hideously lacking in memory," perspica-
ciously reflected on another beneficial aspect of a weakened
memory, one that if we all suffered from it would contribute
much to the peace of the world: "I find some consolation, also, in
the reflection that I have, in the words of a certain ancient author,
a short memory for the injuries I have received. Like Darius, I
should need a prompter. Wishing not to forget the insult he had
suffered from the Athenians, the Persian king made one of his
pages come and repeat three times in his ear, each time he sat
down to table: 'Sire, remember the Athenians'; and it consoles
me too that the places I revisit and the books I reread always smile
upon me with the freshness of novelty."

I was reminded of this "freshness of novelty" when in 2003 I
visited the Church of San Antonio de la Florida in Madrid to
view Goya's frescoes depicting the miracle of Saint Anthony of
Padua. I was told that I had been there to view these frescoes ten
years previously but did not recall having done so. Now, lying on
the floor of the church, I looked up at the painted dome, where
dozens of human figures were disporting themselves as Saint
Anthony raised a man from the dead, and then at the lower vaults
of the church, where the figures of beautiful, diaphanous, rose-
hued female angels were drawing back white cloudlike curtains
to reveal the miracle taking place on the dome—angels aptly de-

scribed by Robert Hughes in his book on Goya as "young actresses in angelic drag. They float and flutter their rainbow wings like butterflies." Absorbing all of this, I was transported up into the church's ether with that inspired feeling of one who sees something for the first time, whether or not one has had a memory of having seen it before. As the French philosopher Gaston Bachelard wrote: "Everything that begins in us with the distinctness of a beginning is a madness of life." One should observe all masterpieces in such a fashion, which is what in fact masterpieces allow us to do; and for this no memory is necessary.

Let us, however, give Mnemosyne her due. Because of her I am able to remember inspiring and rapturous communal moments—for example, the Free Speech Movement rallies in Berkeley, California, in 1965 or the gathering in Central Park in 1980 commemorating the death of John Lennon—as well as passionate and numinous personal moments (and also, of course, sad ones and ones I regret) throughout most of the years not affected by my ECT-induced memory loss. It would have been insuperable for me to have forgotten lying flat on my back with arms outspread on a field filled with wooly yarrow, buckwheat, and live forever overlooking the Pacific Ocean swelling against sculptured rocks in Northern California on a glorious autumn afternoon, or many nights spent in a lake cottage in western Massachusetts watching the lake's ineffable changes as moon and clouds and stars passed by overhead and noticing the traveling lights of fireflies and tiny planes and their reflections in the water. I remember thinking: Like the flickering stars, the firefly's light leaves a memory of itself.

It is said that memory is a reconstruction of people, places, and events, and that one actually remembers the *reconstruction* of these people, places, and events; moreover, memories in the brain are often transformed, so that what you think you are remembering may be something that you are misremembering or imagining. (It is interesting that cognitive scientists suggest we do not perceive the world as it truly is but rather actively construct both it and ourselves.) So I am always overjoyed when trying to reconstruct or imagine friends I once knew at specific times and memorable places in my disappeared world (as, in a way, we all do). In his beautiful song "No Woman, No Cry," Bob Marley sings of the good friends he has had and lost: "In this great future, you can't forget your past / So dry your tears, I say."

What subsists for people who have forgotten their past and/or their present? In a letter to Oliver Sacks concerning the case of Jimmie G., A. R. Luria wrote: "But a man does not consist of memory alone. He has feeling, will, sensibilities, moral being— matters of which neuropsychology cannot speak. . . . Neuropsychologically there is little or nothing you can do; but in the realm of the Individual there may be much you can do." Sacks himself talks of the "living flow or inner music of even the most fragmented individuals" and suggests that his task is the finding and evoking of a "living personal center, an 'I,' amid the debris of neurological devastation."

In one of my files, I discovered an unremembered note, written by myself to myself in one of the hospitals where I was staying during my two-year sojourn in the world of illness and electroshock:

> Look at things dispassionately but intensely in considering personal growth in opening up to new possibilities and stay true to your vision or view in delineating your new outlook. For instance, hold on to the view of a new project, even if you cannot remember, and see the way it defines itself fully no matter where it takes you. But I haven't decided where to go with it or what to explore.
>
> Today I was explaining as best I could to a visiting friend that the shock treatments put on hold much feeling and thought, even dismissing thought and making one forget its reality. Just the barest essentials remain for my consideration, along with daydreams and fantasies that force themselves to my attention. I am living in the moments of my days these days—the long thoughts and feelings more cut down to manageable lengths. I must learn to live in the present. Begin at zero. Start here.

ACKNOWLEDGMENTS

Gratitude is the heart's memory.

—French proverb

I am inestimably grateful to my editors, Ileene Smith and Stephanie Higgs; to my literary agent, Sarah Lazin; to my first reader, Annie Druyan; to my teacher and friend Eileen Mullin; to Richard Gere for his loyalty and support; and to those persons at Random House who helped make this book possible: Jonathan Karp, Luke Epplin, Robin Rolewicz, Evan Camfield, Susan M. S. Brown, and Allison Saltzman. Special thanks to Scott Moyers, who originally suggested and had confidence that I could write this book: *ad astra per aspera.*

Heartfelt thanks to the following persons for their suggestions, encouragement, and inspiration throughout the writing of my book: Wivika Ramel, Philippe Goldin, Jonathan Demme, Joanne Howard, Studs Terkel, Linda Andre, Carey Lowell, Alice Waters, Uma Thurman, Hope Malkan, Dina Haidar, Kimberly Poppe, Isa Ruiz de la Prada, Luis Alaejos, Laura Garcia-Lorca, Amy Kephart Ryan, Tara and Daniel Goleman, Michele and Larry Sacharow, Natalia Gil, Shirley Sun, Dan Solomon, Tom Luddy, Monique Montgomery, Sydney Picasso, Olga Liriano, Julia Hillman, Nina Bengtsson, Petra and Jonas Olsson, Paula Schott, Erika Strömqvist, Raymond Foye, Clinton Heylin, Doris del Castillo, Hanna Wolski, Hanny El Zeini, Sharon Salzberg, Krishna Das, Elizabeth Garnsey, Laetitia d'Ornano, Cathy and Salvatore Trentalancia, Panteha Razavi, Lina von Seth, Paula von Seth, Calle Dierker, Jane Wenner, Jann Wenner, Charlotte Hamilton, Hugo Berch, James Cott, Patrick Cott, Thomas Cott.

N.B.: My comments on and opinions about electroconvulsive therapy are not necessarily those of any of the persons I have interviewed in *On the Sea of Memory*.

About the Author

JONATHAN COTT is the author of fifteen previous books, which have been translated into ten languages, among them *Pipers at the Gates of Dawn: The Wisdom of Children's Literature, The Search for Omm Sety, Isis and Osiris, Conversations with Glenn Gould, Thirteen: A Journey into the Number, Wandering Ghost: The Odyssey of Lafcadio Hearn, Back to a Shadow in the Night: Music Writings and Interviews: 1968–2001,* and three collections of poems, *City of Earthly Love, Charms,* and *Homelands.* He is the editor of *The Roses Race Around Her Name: Poems from Fathers to Daughters* and *Beyond the Looking Glass: An Anthology of Victorian Fairy Tale Novels, Stories, and Poems.* He has been a contributing editor of *Rolling Stone* magazine since its inception and has written for *The New York Times, Parabola,* and *The New Yorker.* He lives in New York City.

About the Type

This book was set in Electra, a typeface designed for Linotype by W. A. Dwiggins, the renowned type designer (1880–1956). Electra is a fluid typeface, avoiding the contrasts of thick and thin strokes that are prevalent in most modern typefaces.